VINTAGE CRICKETERS

VINTAGE CRICKETERS

E. M. WELLINGS

London
GEORGE ALLEN & UNWIN
Boston   Sydney

George Allen & Unwin (Publishers) Ltd,
40 Museum Street, London WC1A 1LU, UK

George Allen & Unwin (Publishers) Ltd,
Park Lane, Hemel Hempstead, Herts HP2 4TE, UK

Allen & Unwin Inc.,
9 Winchester Terrace, Winchester, Mass 01890, USA

George Allen & Unwin Australia Pty Ltd,
8 Napier Street, North Sydney, NSW 2060, Australia

First published in 1983

British Library Cataloguing in Publication Data

Wellings, E. M.
    Vintage cricketers.
1. Cricket
I. Title
796.35'8'0924   GV917
ISBN 0–04–796066–3

Set in 11 on 13 point Garamond by Nene Phototypesetters Ltd
and printed in Great Britain
by Butler & Tanner Ltd, Frome and London

Contents

Illustrations

Preface

While walking through the Hampshire town in which we live I overheard a woman say to another, pityingly, 'Of course, he's seventy-odd you know.' Poor old buffer! Of course that would explain everything, his eccentricities, his obstinacy, his stupidity, and so on and so on. But dash it, I suddenly realised, they could be referring to me. If I'm ever to publish my reminiscences and experiences, mainly about sport and particularly cricket, I'd better get cracking.

In fact, this is not a first attempt. I did write it some years back. I had had six books published. One, I think, was good, the others so-so. The would-be seventh, I was sure, was the best. Of a modest bunch perhaps, but still the best. It did not appeal to a certain publisher. His expert reported that the book 'does not tell us much about the author'. The poor inquisitive fish. It was not meant to. Wellings is of interest essentially to himself. His is a walking-on part.

On a personal note, however, there is one matter I should like to make clear, since it was apparently obscure during the 36 years I was on the *Evening News*. I am of the masculine gender. When I retired I received a letter from the Managing Director, with five mistakes on the envelope, thanking *Mrs* Wellings for her work over the years. Yes, 36 of them, and I never learned to curtsey!

I have often failed to unearth details about certain players of the past, or been unable to construct worthwhile pictures of them. George Lohmann, for instance, the great Surrey bowler, took 112 Test wickets at under 11 runs each. We know his attack was based on off-spin, and we know he was not slow. He was somewhere in the medium range, but whether his basic speed was around fast-medium or slow-medium, a difference of several miles per hour, I have not discovered.

During my more active days there were many interesting and exciting cricketers, about whom future enthusiasts may ask similar questions. They are the characters of wide interest, the cricketers with whom or against whom I played, and some others often seen from the boundary. They were the characters of the rejected book. They are again my characters, but just in case there are one or two others with a strange wish to know something about the author, this will be slightly closer to the popular conception of an autobiography. So enter Wellings, unobtrusively. But I still insist that he is an extra, who was lucky enough on the playing field to meet many grand players, headed by Jack Hobbs, his sporting idol for more than half a century.

VINTAGE CRICKETERS

1

From Quaife to Pataudi

Nearly 40 years separated the youngest and oldest players in first-class cricket, when I made my first tentative approach to that company in 1928. The Nawab of Pataudi was little past his eighteenth birthday, almost exactly a year younger than myself. W. G. Quaife, Willie Quaife, was 56. He played only once that summer, but he ended his long career with Warwickshire as he had started it, with a hundred. Long before Pataudi and I were born, indeed before Warwickshire joined the first-class counties, Quaife scored his first county century in his first match, against Durham. Now, 35 years later, he did the same against Derbyshire in his last.

Players of his generation were long-lasting in all games. James Braid was approaching 60 midway between the wars, when he contested the final of the *News of the World* golf tournament, the big match-play event of the season. A footballer named Meredith played first division League football into his fifties. It was not that the old-timers necessarily retained their playing skills longer than the more modern players. It was rather that their early upbringing so hardened them, particularly in the leg, that they had the endurance to play much longer. They, and my generation also, used their legs as a main means of transport,

1

starting with tramps to school, for there were no buses for them then. To walk became so natural that Harold Larwood used to walk to and from the Sydney ground each day of a Test. Three miles before play, the equivalent of 20 to 30 six-ball overs, and a final three miles on foot built his appetite for dinner. Today fleets of cars carry the players everywhere on tour, to golf courses, to social functions and – incidentally – cricket grounds.

The long playing lives of those stalwarts allowed my generation a wonderful advantage. We could watch and learn from cricketers who had helped to make the period leading to the Great War in 1914 the Golden Age of cricket. I played with or against a score and more who established their fame before that war. They included Jack Hobbs, Sydney Barnes, Wilfred Rhodes and George Gunn, who were playing Test cricket before I was born, and Frank Woolley, who played his first Test in 1909, the year of my birth.

How much the young players of the present would have benefited from similar experiences. Had David Gower been able to study a left-handed batsman such as Woolley early in his career, his development would surely have been much more rapid. He would have seen demonstrated the footwork needed to turn his great natural talent to the fullest advantage long since. If Graham Gooch in his formative years could have studied Patsy Hendren hooking, he might now be playing that stroke more safely from a square-on position. If Derek Underwood had watched Rhodes, he would have been encouraged to develop more of the arts and crafts needed to compete with perfect batting conditions. If today's numerous open-chested quick bowlers had enjoyed the spectacle of such as Barnes and J. T. Hearne, with their lovely sideways actions, the standard of such bowling in England now would be better – and faster.

In 1919 I saw county cricket for the first time and was firmly hooked for all time on the game by Woolley. That was the season of two-day matches with very long hours. Hampshire entertained Kent at Bournemouth, and in 150 minutes Woolley contributed 134 to a Kent win. He also took four wickets with his left-arm spinners. Like Colin Blythe before him, Woolley brought his left arm into the delivery from behind his back. As a small boy at prep school in Bournemouth I copied that method for a time. Then I tried a double-windmill action, which was favoured by Percy Fender, though I had not seen him yet, before developing my final more general method.

It would have been difficult for a youngster already much attracted to cricket not to become hooked as a result of that match. Here was not only Woolley, long and lazily lissom, but also Tich Freeman perkily bobbing up to the stumps to spin his way to a dozen wickets, and the ever-resolute Phil Mead long enduring on behalf of the heavily defeated Hampshire side. There was the colourful scene, the rustic pavilion and the gleaming white tents around the Dean Park ground ringed by elegant houses. There was also the colour brought to the play by the caps worn by amateurs. They included the most beautiful of all cricket caps, the quartered Oxford Harlequin, which was made famous by Plum Warner and Douglas Jardine among others. It was worn that day by B. G. von B. Melle of Hampshire, a South African whose son played for that country as a quick bowler after the second world war.

Cricketers are met at various unexpected times and places. In 1920 I travelled to Egypt, where I had spent most of my first six years, for the summer holiday from school with my family. Two weeks to Port Said from Tilbury, via Gibraltar and Marseilles, on the *Kaiser-i-Hind*, gave me four weeks in Alexandria, after which I was collected for the return journey, again by the *Kaiser-i-Hind*. She spent nearly four weeks reaching Bombay, her turn-round port; 26 years later we were reaching Australia from Tilbury in 21 days. On my outward journey the cabin steward in my part of the ship was James Stone, who pre-war had been Hampshire's wicket-keeper and one of their leading batsmen. At Easter a few months earlier I had become the first boy ever to be coached on the Southampton ground. At that time the net pitches were sited in front of the pavilion, and there I was coached by Jesse Hopkins, a player with Warwickshire and then

3

Hampshire's groundsman. The county players had not yet reported for practice, but Stewart Boyes, the left-arm spinner about to make his mark, was present. He trundled the ball gently but accurately to me, so that I learned more about defence than attack. That I believe to be the wrong way round, but I know I did benefit from that coaching.

How much any of us benefited from another coaching session at that time I do not know. Our headmaster announced that a former Kent captain was to spend two days with us coaching the cricketers. Jerry Weigall arrived, and that will evoke a grin from anyone old enough to remember that most eccentric member of an eccentric Kent cricketing family. He was a grand character but not to be taken too seriously. He proclaimed three maxims. Never run to cover on a hard pitch and never eat pie at a cricket match were two. I remember only that the third was equally inconsequential. In after years Weigall, who was Jerry to old and young alike, was often to be seen after close of play at Lord's surrounded by young members of the ground staff. He found a use for his rolled umbrella demonstrating strokes. On one occasion he brought the gamp down firmly on the top hat of a passing member.

Jerry prefaced our coaching with a talk. In the course of it he told us how important it was to garden, to remove loose objects from the pitch. There were plenty of those, for our nets behind the school were surrounded on three sides by needle-shedding pine trees. I bowled the first ball, straight but otherwise innocuous, which Jerry surely did not get properly in his sights, and bowled him middle stump. He was not a whit disconcerted. He moved a couple of yards down the pitch, removed a pine needle and said, 'There, that'll show you how important gardening is.' I doubt if anything ever put him out of countenance, not even when he overlooked his own first maxim by running to cover in the 1892 University match. He ran out three Cambridge batsmen, including his skipper, Stanley Jackson. He went on to score 63 not out, having gone in at no. 3, but his running contributed importantly to an Oxford victory. Jerry was a joke, but a very pleasant one, and everyone had a soft spot for him. Except the three victims of his rash running, perhaps.

From Weigall to George Dennett was to move from the slightly ridiculous to the almost sublime. Dennett came to Cheltenham College just in time for my arrival on the scene of the 1st XI nets. He was the ideal, sympathetic school coach, who turned us into a decidedly good school side in 1927, with good results until the final encounter, with Haileybury at Lord's. The ground there was so wet at the toss that the coin finished on its edge. Although our side was uppermost, it was not obvious enough, and the re-toss went against us. So did the match, with an innings to spare. It included my busiest playing day ever. On the heavy pitch, as a medium-paced spinner I bowled 36 out of the 40 overs from the pavilion end, and in the remaining 165 minutes of that day carried my bat through our innings. In that long time I made only 44 but can plead that the pitch had become more lively and that we were soon deep in trouble. My busy match ended with an innings of 34 in the follow-on.

Not the least lesson we learned from Dennett was the importance of a smart turn-out. He even had his own special preparation to impart a shiny finish to his buckskin boots, and the brown leather welts were similarly well polished. Playing for Oxford a year later, I came up against Charlie Parker, Dennett's bowling partner for many years in the Gloucester-shire side. Both were left-arm spinners, and together they were responsible for taking nearly 5500 wickets in first-class cricket. Yet such was the quality of that bowling in their time, the list headed by Blythe and Rhodes, abetted by Woolley, that Dennett never played for England and Parker once only. I saw Parker at close quarters, for in the second innings of a match doomed to be drawn I was sent in first with Pataudi. Parker opened the bowling with in-swingers to a tight leg-side field. When the score was 44 for 2 I was still there with 26. Bev Lyon, the Gloucestershire captain, asked me how the light was.

'Fine, thank you,' I replied.

'You've missed the point,' he told me. 'If you appeal against the light now, we'll be able to catch an earlier train.'

However reluctant, a colt with L plates up had to comply. The umpires also welcomed an earlier train, and that was that.

Parker was not a bowler who took kindly to fielding lapses. Typical was his reaction when an opponent pushed the ball down the pitch and past him. At mid-off and mid-on were two elderly fielders whose movements were creaky, Alfred Dipper and Percy Mills. Dipper looked at Mills; Mills looked at Dipper; both started together and reluctantly in pursuit of the ball. Parker in disgust turned to the umpire. 'Look at my bloody whippets,' he said.

Charlie Parker was no batsman, but he was one of a large number of cricketers who have been also fine golfers. At that time he had a handicap of plus three at a club near Cheltenham; Cleeve Hill, I fancy it was. Most of the other good cricketer-golfers were batsmen or all-rounders. The best was surely Leonard Crawley, England's leading amateur golfer in the 'thirties. Ted Dexter with greater application could well have challenged that assessment. Perhaps he was too casual and inclined to change his enthusiasms but, whatever held him back, Dexter never quite made the most of his exceptional talents both at cricket and golf. Of the same generation Tom Graveney has been a fine golfer in the scratch range.

Hammond played in that game at Oxford and made 53, but I never felt he was eager to score heavily against University bowling. Dipper was the top scorer with 110. It was most disconcerting to bowl at old Dip. My run started directly behind the place where I would bowl the ball. From there I moved out in a slight curve. It was, in fact, an upside-down new-moon approach to the wicket. As I started the run I looked down at the ground until I was a couple of paces short of the crease. When I looked up on this occasion, the stumps had disappeared. My immediate thought was that the wicket-keeper had taken leave of his senses and whipped the stumps out of the ground. I stopped, Dipper moved back, and the stumps were revealed again. As the bowler approached, Dipper used to shuffle across the pitch until he was entirely in front of the wicket. Unless you kept an eye on him all the time it was difficult to know where the target was.

In the next match, against Derbyshire, my batting was again better than my bowling, and it was the latter which the skipper wanted. I dropped out, and not surprisingly for I had taken only two very costly wickets, and those at the expense of tail-enders, Parker and Harold Elliot, the Derbyshire wicket-keeper. During that Derbyshire match I was taken on one side by Garnet Lee, the all-rounder, who was their top scorer and, with his leg-breaks, also top wicket-taker. So far as bowling was concerned his advice was the most valuable I ever received.

'You won't take wickets in this class of cricket until you get more pace off the pitch,' he began.

I was puzzled and asked how I should go about it. Nip off the pitch, he stressed, came from getting the body swinging into the delivery. Lee, who began in the Nottinghamshire side before the Great War, told me my action was good but I was bowling mainly with the arm unsupported by the body.

It was standard practice at that time for senior players to advise and help the youngsters. In some ways I learned more from such talks during matches than I did in the nets. The next season, when I had contributed to an innings defeat of Northamptonshire on a rude pitch at Wellingborough, I was taken aside by Vallance Jupp. He was then captain of Northamptonshire, having made his mark during the Golden Age with Sussex and also played for England. He too was an all-rounder who bowled off-breaks. He lectured me on field placing. When going round the wicket to bowl off-breaks I used to have three fielders at short leg, a mid-on and two on the boundary at long-on and mid-wicket. Jupp insisted that I needed a third deep behind square leg instead of a mid-on. I was not entirely convinced, but when next bowling in comparable conditions I placed the extra deep fielder. He took two catches, and I was entirely convinced.

After Lee's talk I watched bowlers with a new interest. Sure enough, all the wicket-takers had the body well back approaching the crease and got it 'in back' – as the Americans graphically put it – of the arm swing. That was true of the slow spinners, Rhodes, Parker, Jupp, Freeman, Woolley and the rest. It was particularly noticeable in the faster bowlers. Ted McDonald was still the best of the expresses. He had the most glorious action: a smooth easy run, full of rhythm, leading to an effortless explosion at the crease. I watched him on a true Oxford pitch bringing the ball back three to four inches from the off. He was not the fastest, but certainly the best, fast bowler I ever saw and, though he was quite a heavy drinker, the excellence of his method enabled him to retain his speed and skill so long that at the age of 38 he topped 100 wickets.

The bowler with the most pronounced body action was Maurice Tate, the prince of fast-medium bowlers. As his right foot went forward towards the bowling crease, his body was inclined back at an angle of about 30 degrees from the vertical and everything went into the delivery. This gave him such nip off the pitch that he was made for the lightning Australian pitches of that era, pitches based on Bulli soil. In 1924–25 Tate took 38 wickets in the five Tests, still a record for England in Australia. There was one side effect of his success there. Once he acquired the ideal length for Australian pitches he had difficulty re-adjusting to English conditions. He subsequently tended to pitch rather too short. Hence he was not quite so dangerous, but it was very difficult to score fast against him.

In his time wicket-keepers stood up to bowlers of almost any pace, but Tate's haste off Australian pitches disconcerted Herbert Strudwick. In an aggrieved tone of voice he once said, 'He was so quick off, faster than our fast bowler Gilligan, that I had to stand *back* to him with the new ball.'

Cricketers of his era were not encouraged to be demonstrative. Players left it to spectators to do the applauding, and they showed no excitement at the capture of a wicket. They were not expected to show their feelings when narrowly missing a wicket. Tate was regarded as a special case. He did throw up his arms on such occasions, and in one or two other ways showed feelings of anticipation or disappointment. He was such a cheerful soul, large and pleasantly round of face, that he was known widely as 'Chubby' Tate, and could be forgiven anything. When he retired in the late 'thirties he joined us for a time in the press box. Later he became a publican, but in that capacity he had no chance of prospering. His hail-fellow-well-met disposition caused him to stand drinks for anyone he knew who entered the pub. He treated the profits away.

Tate was the more modern counterpart of Surrey's Tom Richardson, one of the game's greatest fast bowlers. They were tireless cricketers of great heart, putting everything into their game, and both had runs of astonishing success. In four English seasons from 1894 Richardson took 1005 wickets, and his average work-load was the equivalent of 1375 six-ball overs a season. While exceeding 200 wickets in three successive seasons from 1923 Tate bowled even more. He averaged 1591 overs a season, which by modern standards of productivity is astounding. Moreover, at that time Tate was regularly doing the all-rounder's double. Those men who matured in the Golden Age were certainly hard. Before the Great War and afterwards until the middle of the 1922 season Tate was a slow spin-bowler. The change came by chance. Sussex were in the nets, and he was bowling to Arthur Gilligan. Suddenly he let go a quick one and shattered the wicket. When a few more had proved equally difficult to play, Gilligan persuaded him to adopt pace as his regular method, and he was immediately very successful.

How long, I wonder, would it have been before I learned about producing nip off the pitch, which was the kernel of bowling success, and particularly Tate's, if Garnet Lee had not taken me on one side to help me? Lee opened the way for me to play regularly for Oxford in the following season (1929) and greatly extend my familiarity with the play and the ways of the top cricketers.

2
Yorkshire
wits and wiles

Before Oxford's second match of 1929 a large shiny limousine stopped in Parks Road outside Wadham College while the driver asked the way to The Parks. I was also on my way there and was invited to 'hop in'. An unusual introduction to York-shire cricket. The driver, Captain William Worsley, said 'Of course, you know who's in the back.' Certainly, it was Wilfred Rhodes, very easily recognised but not so easily understood, for he had the softest Yorkshire voice imaginable. His audience strained to hear him.

It was perhaps significant that the team's skipper should be acting as the chauffeur, while his senior professional was spread at his ease in the back seat. Why not the front seat? Most puzzling, but perhaps this illustrated something about current Yorkshire cricket. It was going through a rather difficult period of transition. In the later 'twenties senior professionals tended to take advantage of weak captaincy. Their behaviour was not always worthy of the county, and in 1924 it exceeded the bounds at Sheffield when Middlesex were the visitors. Middlesex left the ground determined not to play Yorkshire in 1925, though they did relent after the results of an official inquiry were published. Abe Waddington, the fast-medium left-arm bowler, was named as the main offender. Bad blood unfortunately long marred Yorkshire–Middlesex relations. The initial fault lay undoubtedly with Yorkshire, but subsequently I felt that Middlesex were mainly to blame for the feud being allowed to continue through the 'thirties.

Emmott Robinson, middle-order batsman and out-swing bowler of lively medium pace from a jaunty, bouncy run, was another inclined to step out of line. At this time Yorkshire were not dismissing opponents as easily as they expected, which was perhaps why there were occasions when those fielding close seemed to be more concerned to talk their opponents out. Robinson was one of those foolish enough to talk out of turn while Johnny Douglas was batting for Essex. It was surely a measure of Yorkshire frustration that they should risk the wrath of that particular opponent. Douglas was a middleweight boxer of considerable renown. On that occasion he did some talking back himself. He addressed those around the slips and informed them that any more and he would be waiting for the offenders at close of play. There was no more chat.

Brian Sellers has been widely credited with restoring discipline to Yorkshire cricket in the 'thirties. In fact the work had already been done in 1930 by Alan Barber. He was captain of Oxford in 1929 and of Yorkshire a year later. He could spare only one summer for cricket after finishing at University, but that was enough. Barber benefited from a slight stutter. In most people that would be accounted a handicap; in Barber's case it tended to emphasise anything he said, as though the slight hesitation gave his words added importance. Not even Rhodes, who had long been the real Yorkshire captain, was proof against Barber's determination. The showdown was brief but crucial. At the end of an over Barber intimated that he wanted Rhodes to field at short extra. Rhodes, however, continued his journey to the peaceful haven of mid-on, which he regarded as his preserve. When he arrived and turned round, Barber was standing in the middle of the pitch.

'W-Wilfred,' he said, 'short extra o-or the pavilion.' Rhodes chose short extra.

Herbert Sutcliffe also tried something on when Yorkshire were left with 15 minutes for batting at the end of a day. Sutcliffe remarked that he did not think he would bat that evening. Very quietly and with just the hint of his stutter Barber told him, 'Get your pads on, Herbert.' Herbert batted.

There was great strength of character in Alan Barber. As a cricketer he was a sound, determined opening batsman and a fine fielder, but it was as a leader that he excelled. The pity was that schoolmastering occupied him to the exclusion of cricket. However, he certainly prepared the way for Sellers and, if the latter met with a flicker of initial resistance, he was well equipped to overcome it.

In his first match there was such a flicker. He arrived in the company of his father, a former Yorkshire player, and together they inspected the pitch. After tossing, Brian again talked to his father before returning to the dressing room to announce that Yorkshire were to field. He was quizzed by Macaulay.

'Did you win the toss?' he asked.

'Yes.'

'And you put them in?'

'Yes.'

'Did your father tell you to put them in?'

'Yes.'

'Then tell your father to bloody well come and bowl them out,' Macaulay exploded.

It used to be said that when Yorkshire is strong, England is strong. Before the second world war they usually were strong, and even during their anxieties in the later 'twenties they were regularly at or near the top in the Championship. I have two playing reasons for remembering that 1929 match at Oxford. By one ball I missed being Bill Bowes' first victim as a Yorkshire bowler. That was not his initial first-class match, for he was then on the staff at Lord's and had played for MCC. It was, however, his first county match. Bill appeared to be on the wrong side, for he looked much more like a student than a professional cricketer. He was very large, and he wore very large spectacles. A tuft of hair curled on the top of his forehead which, plus those large goggles, gave him an appearance of innocence. He never really lost it, and it was among his assets. There was nothing innocent about his bowling. Before I arrived at the crease he up-ended the leg stump inadequately defended by Monty Garland-Wells. My leg stump suffered the same fate next ball.

My other reason for remembering that match particularly was the experience later of batting, briefly, against the left-arm spin and guile of Rhodes. His variations of flight left me metaphorically scratching my head and wondering what new form of cricket I had strayed into. After playing back to a half-volley which looked as if it was going to drop short, and forward to a short ball which looked like becoming a half-volley, I was quite lost. Rhodes achieved his flight by varying the position of his left hand when the ball was sent on its way. For the one that looked like developing into a half-volley until it suddenly plunged, he had the back of his hand showing to the batsman.

Three years earlier I had watched Rhodes dismiss Arthur Richardson in the first innings of the 1926 Test at The Oval, where England regained the Ashes. Richardson spooned the ball quietly to George Geary at mid-off. It looked such a soft form of dismissal. After my experience in The Parks I had a different slant on that dismissal. I could understand too how Bob Wyatt of Warwickshire came to miscalculate the bowling of Rhodes. Watching from the pavilion during his first match against Yorkshire, he concluded that, 'You can hit him over mid-on.' Soon after his turn came to bat, he returned to the pavilion and said, 'No, you can't.' He had hit Rhodes over mid-on once. He went to hit him there a second time and was caught at mid-off.

Rhodes approached the wicket at a slant. Most bowlers have their feet in line down the pitch in the delivery stride. Rhodes' right foot landed some dozen inches on the left or, being left-handed, off-side of his left. That gave him a very solid right side against which to do his spinning. The same quality was noticeable in the method of Tom Goddard, the right-hander whose front foot was therefore the left, the opposite of Rhodes. Goddard's left foot came down so turned back on itself that it was pointing towards mid-on. His left side was rigid. Where these two great bowlers differed was in size of hand. Rhodes had hands of normal size; Goddard had enormous dinner-plates.

If chance changed Maurice Tate from a slow to a fast-medium bowler and carried him to greatness, Goddard went in reverse. He set out with Gloucestershire as a fast bowler, for which his great hands seemed so ill-suited that he was under notice, when reprieve came with the discovery of his off-spinning talents.

It is an astonishing fact that 30 years separated the first and last appearances of Wilfred Rhodes in Test cricket. To those who experienced the guile allied to accuracy of his bowling in old age, and who understood the soundness of his batting, which was right-handed, it is not so astonishing. As my generation saw him at the wicket, he played from a very open stance, what was called between the wars a two-eyed stance. In his great batting days as Hobbs' opening partner in Tests, he had played from a square stance. The change, he claimed, helped him to avoid giving slip catches. It is an ugly position, and at first sight it seems to handicap off-side play. Yet we have seen good off-side stroke play from batsmen with similar stances. Rhodes could still drive to the off. More recently Jim Parks – young Jim – adopted a similar stance and was still stronger in attack on the off-side than on the leg.

In his veteran years Rhodes could be a trifle catty. In June of the summer after he retired from the Yorkshire side Ian Peebles met him and asked about his successor, Hedley Verity.

'He's not bad,' said the great man and caused Peebles to prick up his ears by adding, 'He's got one ball I hadn't got.'

'Oh, what's that?' asked Ian.

'It's the one they cut,' he replied scathingly.

If batsmen found the opportunity to cut Verity that spring, he certainly gave them very few opportunities subsequently. Verity was as accurate as ever Rhodes could have been. They were both great bowlers but could not otherwise be compared. Each was a left-handed spin-bowler, but there the similarity virtually ended. The basic pace of Rhodes was slow, that of Verity nearer slow-medium. Size dictated their methods. Rhodes was on the short side, ideally built for tossing the ball into the air and baffling opponents by flight. His slanting approach to the wicket was slow and measured. Verity was much taller, his run to the wicket longer and more brisk. They both practised the arts of deceptive variations in various ways. From his height Verity never attempted the flight variations of his predecessor, but he subtly varied his pace, the length from which he bowled and the direction of his bowling, by using the full width of the crease.

Those were arts learned by all slow and medium-paced bowlers. To us it is strange to see the modern spinners bobbing up time after time to deliver from precisely the same place. The last slow bowler who used those variations was Fred Titmus, and he learned his trade long before the one-day limited-overs game was introduced to put the emphasis fairly and squarely on economy. Titmus learned to bowl, like Rhodes, Verity and their contemporaries, when we were encouraged to trade runs for wickets.

While on the subject of Yorkshire cricket, I can illustrate that from personal experience. In 1931 in The Parks I had the prized wicket of Maurice Leyland off the last ball of an over in which he biffed 14 runs. He lofted a four straight, he lofted a six straight and a second four driven in the same direction. I continued to keep the ball well up to him, trying to deceive him in the air, and he did hit the final ball rather too early. It soared high over the bowler's head and into the safe hands of the fielder beside the sight-screen.

That example points the difference between cricket then and since the introduction of the limited-overs scramble. Tactics for the latter soon dominated thinking in all first-class cricket, for the awarding of bonus points in championship matches rendered the bowling of maidens seemingly more significant than the capture of wickets. The bowler who now squandered with reckless extravagance 14 runs in an over would be summarily dismissed from the attack, even though he also removed a Test batsman in that over. However, it would be wrong to give the impression that between the wars the game was as adventurous as it had been in the Golden Age. Fielders in the deep were still used and bowlers were still willing to trade runs for wickets, but clearly not to the same extent as in 1914.

In his old age Rhodes lost his sight. Yet he continued to attend cricket matches, his ears telling him something of the play and a friend augmenting his knowledge. When Hampshire visited Yorkshire, their left-arm slow bowler, Peter Sainsbury, was brought on. Rhodes asked what field he had. His interpreter told him.

'Nobody in the deep by the sight-screen?' asked Rhodes.

'No.'

'Must be bowling badly,' was his terse summing-up. Yes, bowling badly by the standards of Rhodes' day, but surely doing just what the modern skipper wanted.

One Yorkshire slow bowler of those days would have been in his element today. Horace Fisher would surely have been the logical successor to Rhodes had his wicket-taking ambitions been greater. In fact he was always more interested in keeping his opponents quiet than in dismissing them. It was said by his Yorkshire colleagues that at any time he could say how many overs he had bowled for how many runs. Fisher played on occasions for the county, but he remained essentially a League cricketer.

Yorkshire possessed amazing depth of class left-arm bowling in those days. Rhodes retired, Verity followed and speedily became a Test bowler, and behind him was the admirably steady but unambitious Horace Fisher. In 1946 we learned that there was yet another left-arm spinner of lofty class parked in the wings all that time. At the age of 43 Arthur Booth took

111 wickets at 11.6 each and helped the county to win yet another championship. He had previously played once only for Yorkshire and did most of his pre-war county work in the Northumberland side among the Minor Counties.

Our standards between the wars were set by the Yorkshiremen. They were so monotonously at the top that inevitably their few defeats were vastly applauded. That is not the same as saying that any of us – except perhaps some in Middlesex – wished them ill. I found the Yorkshiremen of my period a magnificent bunch. They played cricket hard, but not to the exclusion of chivalry. Off the field they were splendid companions. Personally, I preferred Yorkshire as opponents to any other county. A modicum of success against Yorkshire was cause for much rejoicing.

Brian Sellers became captain in 1932. In some ways he took over a side that captained itself, so efficient was it in all branches. When he took over, George Macaulay and Emmott Robinson were still in the attack; Bowes and Verity had already and speedily established themselves in the top flight. Any and all bowling changes were virtually guaranteed to be good ones. In his time, moreover, the side contained auxiliary bowlers liable to break up a dangerous partnership if such an alliance ever developed. Maurice Leyland bowled his left-arm googlies and off-breaks, Hutton his right-arm googlies and leg-breaks. Behind them were a splendid set of fielders, among whom the new skipper and 'Ticker' Mitchell excelled near the bat. With Holmes, Sutcliffe, Oldroyd, Leyland, Mitchell and Wilf Barber to start the batting, runs were never a problem, even before the youthful Len Hutton joined the scorers.

During the 'fifties, when Surrey were winning seven Championships in a row, mainly under the inspiring leadership of Stewart Surridge, the question of the greatest county side of the century was often discussed. I should like to put my own county of Surrey first. Certainly they were the equals of Sellers' Yorkshire in the field, for Bedser, Surridge, Laker and Lock, who were soon joined by Loader, formed a great attack. In the close catching positions also, Yorkshire were rivalled by Surridge himself, the incomparable Tony Lock and Micky Stewart. However, even though Surrey had Peter May at his best, their batting was never as solid and relentless as Yorkshire's in the 'thirties. To me that Yorkshire side was the best ever and how England benefited!

Yorkshire's supporters were not always satisfied by the number of their players in the Test team. During the 'twenties one of them wrote to a cricket periodical – *The Cricketer* I think – suggesting an England team. He named ten Yorkshiremen and, being in a generous mood, yielded one place to Hobbs. But of course, with Holmes and Sutcliffe in the side, Hobbs could not open the innings!

I had tremendous admiration and affection for those Yorkshire stalwarts of the 'thirties. In addition to outstanding playing ability there was great character and wit in the side. Sometimes the humour was dry, as when Leyland summed up the Yorkshire–Lancashire match: 'First morning we say, "How do", afterwards we say only, "How's that?" '

Number one humorist was Arthur Wood, the round little man who succeeded Arthur Dolphin behind the stumps. His face was also round and eternally cheerful. He it was who urged Verity to keep going, telling him he had South African Cameron in two minds after an over which contained three sixes and three fours. When Verity asked him what he was talking about, Wood replied, 'He doesn't know whether to hit you for four or six.' He was the same cheerful character in retirement when playing Sunday charity games for Jack Appleyard in Roundhay Park outside Leeds. There was one particular game in which the recently retired Wally Hammond was the star attraction. He had made seven when he hit the ball high towards the square-leg boundary. From far away an eager young fielder raced towards the ball, heedless of Wood's shouts from behind the stumps to 'leave it alone, miss it,' and brought off a great running catch. Never was fine performance less appreciated.

No less cheerful was the other Arthur, Mitchell, who was

more often known as 'Ticker'. Mitchell was conspicuous in the field by reason of his habit of wearing his cap with the peak slanting across his forehead. At the wicket Mitchell did not look a classic batsman. There was a utility stamp on his play, but there was no question of his soundness, nor of his typically Yorkshire fighting spirit. He had, moreover, a perfect temperament for cricket, which enabled him to take every occasion in his stride.

One such occasion was the 1935 Test match at Leeds against South Africa. On the morning of the match Leyland was stricken by lumbago, and the selectors sought Mitchell. He was at home gardening, but rushed to the ground to play innings of 58 and 72. At the time South Africa had their best attack since the googly days of Schwarz, Faulkner, Vogler and company in the early years of the century.

Yet Ticker's greatest innings was played at Old Trafford in 1933 against the Lancastrian foe. Even in those days, when groundsmen were generally left to get on with the job of preparing the best possible pitch, some foolish experiments were made. Such was the case then in Lancashire, and the result was an indescribably bad pitch. But for Mitchell there would have been little life remaining in the match after the first day. Lancashire disposed of Holmes, Sutcliffe and Leyland, but for more than six hours, while he was making 123, Mitchell's defence was proof against the ball's most extravagant behaviour.

His reward was a slanging for a laborious innings from Neville Cardus in the *Manchester Guardian*. Neville's face was red when events next day indicated that his estimate of the conditions was far wide of the mark, and that Mitchell's innings was a masterpiece. Lancashire were hurried in and out for 93 and 92. Macaulay took 12 wickets, Verity six, and the former regretted that he could not have a third crack at the Lancastrians.

Yorkshire's cricket was ruthlessly efficient but, as indicated, not without chivalry. I was the object of their chivalry in 1931.

19

Dismissed scoreless in the first innings, I had the task of bustling against a pair on a sticky pitch with Macaulay and Verity bowling. Mitchell was at short extra cover. My first ball from Verity found the bat and went in the direction of Mitchell. I shouted, 'Come,' put my head down and raced for the far end. As I slid my bat to safety I looked round to see how my partner had fared. He was safe, and there seemed to have been no commotion at that end either. Mitchell had the ball, tossing it from hand to hand while laughingly enjoying the sight of us racing to avoid my pair. Of course, Yorkshire could afford to be generous; we were at their mercy on that pitch and managed only 80.

Macaulay, I may say, was less magnanimous. Relieved to be off the mark, I hit out hopefully at his bowling. As much by luck as anything else the outcome was a four over mid-off. I was ignorant of how fiercely Macaulay was accustomed to react to an indignity. I pushed forward at the next ball of quite full length, but it was viciously spun at well above medium pace. It reared and turned sharply from the off, struck me high on the chest and knocked me over backwards.

Macaulay was a great cricketer. I use the adjective 'great' while remembering that he played once only for England against Australia and in only eight Tests altogether. The match against Australia was that at Leeds in 1926, when one thing only went right for England – the winning of the toss by Arthur Carr. He gave Australia first innings and, after Tate had summarily dismissed Warren Bardsley, Carr himself dropped Charles Macartney off him four balls later. Macartney then raced to a hundred before lunch, Bill Woodfull and Arthur Richardson added centuries, and the luckless Macaulay emerged with 1 for 123 off 32 overs. The Australians had much respect for Macaulay's bowling. If they could hit him out of the side, that was a gamble worth taking. Fortune was with them. Going in at no. 10 on that occasion, when eight wickets had fallen for 182, Macaulay did, however, help England towards a draw by hitting 76 out of 108.

We are all at our best as fielders off our own bowling. Among the many catches I grounded I recall only two off my own bowling, and they are etched in my memory. The best fielder of all from his own bowling was Macaulay. He was no less belligerent as a fielder than as a bowler. He seemed to pounce with eager relish on anything hit back in his direction. He is the only bowler I ever saw run out an opponent playing a defensive forward stroke with no thought of running. That happened at Oxford in 1929. Hill-Wood pushed the ball back towards Macaulay and allowed his right foot to advance in front of the batting crease. Macaulay pounced and threw down the far wicket before Hill-Wood could return his foot. What a tigerish cricketer George Macaulay was, and what great things he did for Yorkshire despite never enjoying the best of health. Back trouble finally caused his retirement in the middle 'thirties.

Macaulay's name figures in several of the rich Yorkshire stories of the period. He was batting with Herbert Sutcliffe when that maestro was struck a painful blow in the box. Sutcliffe was essentially a showman. He was not likely to muff that chance of occupying the centre of the stage. Soon almost everyone on the field of play was gathered round, commiserating and encouraging him to rub the afflicted parts. All except George Macaulay, who took the opportunity to stretch out on his back at the other end and have a rest. When adequately refreshed, he rose to his feet, advanced four or five paces down the pitch and addressed his partner: 'Herbert, Herbert, stop pleasurin' thaself and get on wit' game.'

As for Sutcliffe, nobody surely in sport has ever capitalised so completely on his talents as Herbert did. He was never the artist that his legendary partner, Jack Hobbs, was, but as a batting machine he was excelled only by Don Bradman. He had the odd fault but understood it and knew how to counter it. When hooking he played much in the air, and opponents sought to capitalise on that apparent weakness. Sutcliffe, however, kept the hook stroke in check until he had the measure of the conditions. Then he reckoned to be able to direct his lofted hooks clear of any lurking fielder and used the stroke freely.

He was also the most imperturbable cricketer. Nothing disturbed the smooth set of his dark hair with its dead straight parting near the centre. Narrow escapes affected him less than water falling on a duck's back. During his epic stand of 172 with Hobbs during the second innings of the 1926 Test, when they played through an Oval sticky, the ball did once reach Sutcliffe's wicket. It trickled against the foot of the stumps to shift a bail, but not hard enough to cause it to fall, which the law then required. Sutcliffe glanced at the wicket, satisfied himself and leaned on his bat facing down the pitch. Behind him the Australians gathered to study the situation. Sutcliffe unconcernedly waited for the commotion to end. The square-leg umpire finally settled the bail back in its groove and Sutcliffe got on with the job. His attitude suggested that, so far as he was concerned, the incident had no significance.

Sutcliffe was an oddity in his time. He was not just a professional cricketer with any fringe earnings coming also from the game; he was a business tycoon and comported himself accordingly. Wilfred Rhodes may have had his skipper chauffeuring for him; Sutcliffe arrived in his own limousine and one still more handsome than that of Worsley. From an early stage in his career he ceased to be the down-to-earth Yorkshireman which his fellow players remained. Even his accents were not those of a Yorkshireman. In truth I am not sure whose they were.

Yet his native shrewdness remained with him throughout. He could have become the first professional to captain Yorkshire, for he was given the chance to succeed before Sellers. Wisely, he reckoned the time was not yet ripe for professional captains. He expressed gratitude to the committee for the offer and, while declining it, affirmed his willingness to play under anyone they might appoint. His was surely the general attitude of those who were playing for a living. They did not wish to be saddled with the extra responsibility of captaincy, except from behind the scenes when the ultimate responsibility was not theirs.

Much has been made of the different dressing rooms and different gates used by the professionals and amateurs at that time. This was not a matter of snobbery but one of sound common sense. The professional was engaged throughout the summer. He needed his own niche, and he found it in the dressing room reserved for professionals. There he was free from the inconvenience of casual amateurs, who might be in for a couple of games and out for the next half-dozen, trespassing on his preserve. There also he was free to express his view of the amateur skipper and of his county's management without being overheard.

Different gates for amateurs and professionals were by no means common. There were different ones at Lord's, because the two dressing rooms were far apart. The professionals had the best of that deal. They could step almost straight from their dressing room onto the playing area. The amateurs had to walk down the stairs, through the long room of the pavilion and finally down the steps in the centre of the pavilion. The next man in could not lose much time if he was to be at the wicket within two minutes of the wicket falling.

It should also be stressed that different dressing rooms were the practice only on headquarter grounds. On the smaller ones amateurs and professionals shared the same dressing room. Moreover, even on the big grounds meals were taken together.

There was no more stirring sight in cricket than that of Maurice Leyland going to bat when his side was in difficulties. His short, square figure advancing to the wicket exuded confidence. It did not look as if he could possibly fail in such circumstances, and he rarely did. Just to see him walk onto the field gave us faith that all would now come right. In the middle and late 'thirties Leyland's was the English wicket the Australians were most eager to take. Given the choice of Hammond's or Leyland's, they would have chosen the latter. England v. Australia was the peak of cricket, and the higher Leyland went the more successful he was. His county average was around 40, his Test average altogether 46, but against Australia it was 56.8. In his last 11 Tests against Australia he hit no fewer than six centuries and averaged almost 70 an innings.

Astonishingly, Leyland was used only once in 1938. There was one Test in which he could not have played, that at Leeds, which closely followed a meeting disastrous for England between Middlesex and Yorkshire at Lord's. On a spiteful, rain-affected pitch Hutton suffered a broken finger, Leyland a broken thumb and Paul Gibb, who with Les Ames out of action with a bad back was England's first-choice stumper, a head injury. England lost the low-scoring Test at Leeds, in which Bowes and Verity were Yorkshire's only representatives. They had five in the triumphant side at The Oval a month later and accounted for 612 runs and 10 of the 16 wickets which fell to the bowlers.

Leyland's other absences that summer were due to the selectors. It was claimed that he had trouble in his left shoulder which handicapped him in throwing from the deep. What a piffling excuse for overlooking the most consistently successful Test batsman in the country! When he did come in at The Oval, Leyland set England a long, long way towards the eventual overwhelming victory by hitting 187 and sharing a second wicket stand of 382 with Hutton.

The history of English Test cricket during the past 60 and more years is studded with inexplicable selection decisions, of omission and commission alike. The list could be started with the overlooking of George Gunn immediately after the first world war. Gunn was in his element against fast bowling, but the selectors chose numerous apprehensive characters instead to tackle Gregory and McDonald. One of those characters brought off a well-struck late cut from which the leg stump was levelled by the ball! Batting on the retreat, which was never Gunn's way.

It is curious how often victims of selectorial blunder have been northerners, and particularly Yorkshiremen. Not long before the Leyland omission, Gubby Allen's team was crippled in Australia by the absence of Bowes and Lancastrian Eddie

Paynter. England, with the rub of the green in their favour, won the first two Tests and reached a winning position in the fourth, which the two northerners might well have clinched. England had not enough bowling support for Bill Voce and relied overmuch on three batsmen, Hammond, Leyland and Charlie Barnett.

Four years earlier Paynter, who excelled, like Leyland, when things were going badly, had been a conspicuous success in Australia under Douglas Jardine. In the season before the next touring side was launched he exceeded 2000 runs and averaged 45.8. Of the tourists only Hammond, Laurie Fishlock and Leyland had better averages. To prefer Derbyshire's Sam Worthington to Paynter was madness in an acute form. Bowes had also been in Australia with Jardine. He learned much then and by 1936, when his 123 wickets cost only 13.4 each, he was a much improved bowler. Skipper Allen was said to have been the selector who turned the thumb down on Bowes and Paynter. He paid a heavy price by losing the series 3–2. He was also skipper in the three Tests against India in 1936 when the touring team was being chosen. Nineteen Englishmen figured in those matches; amazingly Bowes and Paynter were not among them.

Leyland and Verity were the only Yorkshiremen in the 1936–37 series. The former had ample opportunity to show his mettle when his side was in trouble. In the third Test England needed 689 for victory. They had lost six wickets for 195 when Walter Robins joined Leyland – 'only' 494 wanted. Robins had collected a first-innings duck and was bustling. A sharp single avoided the pair, and for a time he continued to take such runs. That was not to the liking of Leyland. At the end of an over he walked down the pitch and urged his partner to 'Take it a bit more quietly; we've got all day tomorrow for getting these runs.' Perhaps not even Leyland the optimist expected to get them, but he and Robins did put on 111 and Leyland went through undefeated, also with 111.

Bill Bowes was the Yorkshireman I knew best. We were

thrown together at various times. After he had so rudely dislodged my leg stump in 1929, our next meeting almost ended similarly. He was then playing for MCC. His first ball to me passed over the middle stump. He was another of those fast-medium bowlers who came unexpectedly fast from the pitch. For a time in the early 'thirties Bill tried his hand at genuine fast bowling with no shortage of bouncers. Jack Hobbs was moved to protest at their frequency. Patsy Hendren turned out with ear muffs but, knowing his love of and his skill in playing the hook stroke, we took that as one of his amusing gestures.

Bowes soon came to the conclusion that, with his ability to move the ball in the air, and with his very high delivery making the most of his 75 inches to get lift from the pitch, fast-medium was his best pace. He was worth much more than a solitary tour and the 14 Tests he played before war came in 1939. He was really shabbily treated by the generally south-dominated selection committees of the period. Nevertheless, he may be ranked with the very best bowlers of his type during the past half century, which rates him near Tate and Alec Bedser.

He and I next bumped into each other at OCTU in the summer of 1940 in the heart of Wales at Llandrindod Wells. I had been in residence a month and was running the cricket, when Bill Bowes walked into the big hotel which was requisitioned for the OCTU and sat down beside me at tea. Two days later we had a match at Builth Wells, where we arrived to find a splendid mix-up. The Builth Wells secretary had with excessive zeal arranged for two matches on the same day, the other opponents coming from South Wales. Builth wanted the two visiting sides to play each other. Eventually they were persuaded that we had a decidedly strong side and could tackle a combined Welsh side of 18 with 11 to field.

By the time we took the field, word had gone round the little town that a Test bowler was about to perform. There were quite 400 round the ground to watch Bill. As we walked out to field, Bill wondered what he ought to bowl. I assured him that all those spectators had not gathered to see him bowl donkey drops.

'All right,' he agreed, 'I'll bowl a couple of quick overs and then switch to off-breaks.'

Nobody could have written a better script. Early in his first over the opening batsman edged a four over the slips. The last ball sent his middle stump cartwheeling, and the sound of the gasp which came from 400 throats lives with me still. In the second over Bill took another wicket. This time he neatly removed the off bail, and we recovered it no more than three yards from the pavilion. Builth Wells had never seen anything like it, and they loved it. So I fancy did Bill Bowes, whose switch to off-breaks brought him a final bag of 12 wickets for 50-odd. The 18 were not enough to prevent a comfortable win for Bowes and company.

Just after the war Bill and I met again. I had been invalided out a year from the war's end. Bill had been released from prisoner-of-war camp. Nobody seeing him when he first came home would have backed him to play two more seasons successfully for Yorkshire. He weighed not much more than nine stone, and with eyes sunk far back into his head he looked a wreck. Freddy Brown, another big man who suffered similarly at the hands of the Axis, was in the same shape.

By the summer of 1945 Bill looked normal, and now we met in the press box. He was preparing for journalism with the *Yorkshire Evening News* after his playing career ended. We sat together in the press box at Bramall Lane, Sheffield, where he reported cricket for the first time in the Victory Series between teams representing England and Australia. Fate threw Bill and me together, and not surprisingly ours is a friendship which has had no difficulty in enduring. I always had great respect for his cricket and for Bowes the man.

There have been few, if any, critics as shrewd in the press box. He and Jim Kilburn of the *Yorkshire Post* formed a very knowledgeable team in the Yorkshire box. Kilburn was reporting cricket for half a century, and was himself an excellent club player. There were, of course, occasionally members of the press box in those days who could have made their mark in the county game. Among them was John Kay of the *Manchester Evening News*. He was one of the best amateur batsmen in the Lancashire League in the palmy days of that competition.

One facet of Bill Bowes, rarely revealed even to his friends, was his conjuring. He was a member of the Magic Circle. I saw him perform once for a few of us on board ship during a voyage to Australia. His technique was seemingly to get into a muddle with the cards. Finally, the worried bemused look still on his face and a look of concern behind the spectacles, he brought it all to a successful conclusion.

Once during a game of bridge Bowes made use of his magic to manipulate a pack of cards. Yorkshire were on tour in Jamaica. Bowes was partnered by Arthur Wood against a couple of locals. He dealt one of his opponents the twelve top spades and an outside ace. He gave Wood most of the other powerful cards and sat back to watch the fun caused by Arthur Wood's obvious impatience to start bidding and the even greater excitement of the opponent, who could not sit still and rose to circle the table. Wood made a high bid. The opponent again circled the table, sat down and called seven spades. Knowing Bill, Wood was of course suspicious but said nothing, and the Jamaicans made their lay-down grand slam. Two years afterwards Bowes again saw the lucky card-player. 'Do you remember that marvellous bridge hand I had against you and Arthur Wood? Never had anything else like it.' Nor ever likely to – unless of course he again landed at the same table as Bill Bowes.

I played against most of the Yorkshiremen whose cricket was so outstanding in the 'thirties, though not Hutton and Sellers. His may have been an easy side to skipper, but that is no reason for withholding any credit from Brian Sellers for the triumphs. He was the right man in the right place. He was the blunt, hail-fellow-well-met Yorkshireman with a habit of addressing folk as 'me old cock sparrer'. He had the happy gift of allowing himself to be absorbed into the body of the team while remaining the boss. If he sometimes gave the impression of being a bull in a china shop, he could when necessary act with tact and diplomacy. That quality was needed in his dealings with Lord's, for Middlesex were not willing even in the late 'thirties to bury the hatchet entirely, following the incidents at Sheffield many years earlier.

Brian Sellers was not a classic batsman, but he was very determined and had the guts to stand up to everything. Many of his most valuable innings were played when Yorkshire were most in need of runs. When Ticker Mitchell played his great innings on the Old Trafford dirt track, Sellers importantly contributed 31, more than any Lancastrian managed in the match. I recall his batting when Yorkshire were gaining an improbable win against Essex on a dodgy, brittle pitch at Ilford in 1938. Having been headed on the first innings, Yorkshire were finally set to score 257 on the third day. Few among us gave them a chance of approaching that figure against the spin of Peter Smith and Laurie Eastman. Yet they were home with four wickets in hand, and Sellers supported Hutton's match-winning innings of 93 not out with 49 priceless runs of his own.

Sellers had his share of the humour which lurked beneath the Yorkshire surface. We were playing a press match against a school in Australia during the 1946–47 tour, our side variously a blend of Australians, Arthur Mailey, Bill O'Reilly, Jack Fingleton, Clarrie Grimmett and Dick Whitington among them, and English writers including Bowes, Sellers and Kilburn. On this particular occasion Norman Preston, soon to become editor of *Wisden*, was in the side. He neglected to remove his wrist-watch before going out to field, to the expressed disgust of a rather pompous member of our side. After the lunch interval, and on the prompting of Sellers, ten of the side went out to field wearing wrist-watches and confounded pomposity. I was one 'old cock sparrer' who had plenty of time for Brian Sellers.

By then, of course, Emmott Robinson, Macaulay, Oldroyd and Holmes had retired, but gaps were usually speedily filled. Hutton was on hand to render the loss of Holmes relatively painless. Without being a second Macaulay, Frank Smailes was a versatile all-rounder who could share the new ball with Bowes and, like the latter at Builth Wells, then switch to off-breaks. Another utility player was Cyril Turner. A new off-spinner, not quite so regularly accurate as most Yorkshire bowlers, was Ellis Robinson and, when free from Cambridge commitments, Norman Yardley and Paul Gibb added to the embarrassment of riches at the disposal of the selectors.

That was the Yorkshire which had my great admiration. They were a closely knit people with more local pride than the folk of any other county. For many, including players, success for Yorkshire was more important than success for England, even against Australia. They were securely grouped against the rest of the world. They could criticise their own, but woe betide any outsider who spoke out of turn. The change to recent times, when a series of well advertised internal squabbles has rent the cricket club, is a matter of continual surprise to those of my age who remember a very different Yorkshire. Our Yorkshire always offered a united front to outsiders. If they had any disagreements among themselves, they were well hidden.

I opposed Yorkshire three times. It was hard but very enjoyable and educationally profitable cricketing work. I regarded my bowling against them in 1931 as the best I ever did. In 44 overs, 13 of which were maidens, I took the wickets of Sutcliffe, Leyland and Mitchell for 93. Among those overs was the one in which Leyland hit 14. I played five innings against Yorkshire bowling, top score 28, lowest nought – twice – and was dismissed in turn by Bowes, Rhodes, Leyland, Macaulay and Verity.

3
Gunn, Woolley, Hendren and others

Preconceived ideas are apt to be upset when one is launched into first-class cricket – southern jollity as opposed to northern dourness, for instance. One of the cheeriest groups who visited The Parks midway between the wars were Derbyshire under the captaincy of Guy Jackson, with the kindly Garnet Lee in their ranks. The men from the garden of England, men of Kent and Kentish men, were much more like the popular conception of northerners than southerners. One Sunday morning I went to the King's Arms, the hotel patronised by most visiting professionals, and there 'rescued' Leslie Todd from what was not far removed from a silent wake.

As the period progressed, however, Kent became a more jovial lot. Percy Chapman became captain and there were several bright sparks among the young amateurs who shortly arrived – Brian Valentine, Hopper Levett, Jerry Chalk and Jack Davies. Among the newer professionals Alan Watt was a similar character. It was just before the 1939 war that the Kent side put up an amusing 'black', which ended the custom of the county team appearing in full war-paint on the stage of the theatre where the Old Strollers regularly performed during Canterbury Week. Their appearance was made on the Thursday, Ladies'

Day. On this particular occasion the show was running very late. Having dined and wined, the Kent team arrived at the theatre at the appointed time. They were told they need not return for another 45 minutes, by which time they were somewhat the worse for wear. They changed into cricket garb – well, more or less. When they wobbled onto the stage, the team was not complete. One player failed to negotiate the route from changing room to stage. There was something wrong with the dress of most of them, and most looked thoroughly under the weather. Hopper Levett had overlooked the need to do up his fly buttons – buttons, not zips in those days. Kent at the time were playing Middlesex, and in the audience at the theatre was their fast bowler, Big Jim Smith. He shook like a jelly most of the following day as he recalled the wonderful sight of the storm-tossed Kent crew scattered about the stage.

Yes, buttons were much safer than the modern zip, as a high cricket official from India learned on a visit to England. He was not very familiar with European dress, particularly evening dress, which he had to don for an important dinner. Unfortunately he heaved on the new-fangled – and to him novel – zip too enthusiastically and zipped himself in the tenderest part. He had to be taken to hospital to be unzipped and stitched.

Leslie Todd, only two years older than myself, was the most infuriating, most perverse cricketer of the generation. He should have played many times for England; in fact he never appeared in a Test. When he came to the Kent side in the middle 'twenties, he was projected as a second Woolley. He certainly had all the necessary left-handed skill to fill that role. His stroke play could be as varied and flashing. He did not have the exceptional reach of that master, but he was not otherwise less well equipped. He failed to make the most of his talents because he had the most extraordinary temperament, which was the despair of his skipper, Percy Chapman, in the early 'thirties.

During an end-of-war match at Lord's I was fielding at second slip, between Todd and Chapman, who was in the gully. The ball went down the leg-side off the batsman's pad and Todd chased it almost to the pavilion rails. Chapman set off to back him up.

'What are you doing that for?' I asked. 'Toddie can throw that distance easily enough.'

'Yes, I know he can, but he won't if nobody backs him up,' Chapman asserted. At odd times during that game he expanded on the abstruse subject of Leslie Todd, cricketer extraordinary. If, after Kent had batted for most of a day, Toddie went to bat an hour before the close to score fast, he would quietly play out time, and his side would be lucky to get 15 to 20 runs from him. If he went in with Kent in some trouble and half an hour of the day's play remaining, he was liable to go mad, forget instructions to concentrate on staying there and clout 40 runs.

He was a difficult man to captain, and we had an example of his curious temperament in that one-day game at Lord's. A side representing Middlesex and Essex opposed Surrey and Kent. We had ample time to score some 220 to win, but Toddie so laboured that the later batsmen fell steadily when trying wildly to make up lost time. When I went in, he said he was troubled by something in his left eye, and I asked him why in that case he didn't get out and leave it to someone else. To compound his offence Todd fell at the start of the final over, having long toiled for 79, and Doug Wright, who had earlier taken six wickets, had to play through the remainder of it to save the match.

It sounds as if Toddie would not make friends easily. In fact he was a very pleasant companion and was well liked by several different types of people. We all made allowances for him and grieved that so much exceptional talent, while not exactly going to waste, was not put to better use. Despite his temperament and the loss of the six war years, when he was at his peak, he scored more than 20,000 runs. He was a complete all-rounder. In his early years with the county he bowled slows, and here also he was thought likely to be another Woolley. He did not come along as a spinner, but in the closing seasons before the war he was a left-arm medium-quick bowler with a late in-swinger in the 100 wickets a season class. He did the double, and altogether he took nearly 600 wickets. After the war he suffered from back trouble. Though he continued to score runs, he did little bowling.

The nearest Todd came to representative honours was one appearance in a Test trial, in which he did not come off. Many less talented cricketers have played for their country. A county could include a wayward genius, but Test selectors would have been taking an unwarranted chance by choosing someone whose approach to the job was so unpredictable.

My two county games in 1928 had brought me up against Charlie Parker from the Golden Age and the very helpful Garnet Lee. Thanks to the latter I had a full season in the Oxford side in 1929, meeting more and more of the men of that era, and becoming convinced that cricket must have reached its peak in the years leading to war in 1914.

In a two-day match I had bowled against one of the seven Foster brothers, who had caused Worcestershire to be called Fostershire. He was Geoffrey, who was in four Oxford sides between 1905 and 1908. He was a beautifully fluent batsman who, like so many in that great age, liked to improvise and even invent strokes. That day he scorned to treat an off-side half-volley from me to an orthodox off-drive. He scored four from the ball, but by glancing to fine leg with a well-timed flick of the wrists.

Perhaps I should have been prepared for the unusual from George Gunn, who had two great Test series in Australia before the Great War and was disastrously forgotten in the two immediate post-war series. As usual he opened the innings for Nottinghamshire. I had the new ball for the second over. Gunn flicked the first two to the boundary beyond cover. If nothing else, neither was of a length to merit such treatment. I was quite shaken, and the third ball was a rank long hop. Gunn played it gently back. On that occasion his fancy was to score off good balls and to take no toll of bad ones. His fancies were many and varied. That particular one produced an innings of 86.

A year or so later he played an innings of similar size against Leicestershire, where times of play had recently been changed. In an attempt to attract late-afternoon spectators, play on the first two days was extended into the evening. Meal intervals were accordingly changed. At half-past-one Gunn, still batting, started to walk to the pavilion. He was called back and informed that they did not lunch until 1.45. Gunn returned, left a wide gap through which the next ball bowled him, and again set off for the pavilion. 'I lunch at half-past-one,' he announced on his way out.

In his book, *100 Years of Trent Bridge*, which was published in 1938, E. V. Lucas wrote:

> He is the only batsman I have seen who carried his fancies to the wicket and indulged them there. Ordinary batsmen are true to type, but George, as the fit took him, would be sometimes a hitter, sometimes a stone-waller, sometimes pure virtuoso, when his bat became a wizard's wand, and sometimes, as one of the umpires said, he would go to sleep.

George Gunn had a sense of the fitness of things. On his fiftieth birthday he scored 164 against Worcestershire and did not yield his wicket. At that age also he was very belatedly recalled, together with Wilfred Rhodes, who was nearly two years his senior, to tour the West Indies. He played in all four Tests and had a batting average of 34.5. Only Patsy Hendren, Andy Sandham and Les Ames made more runs than his 276.

His fancy at one stage of that tour was to 'take the mickey' out of Learie Constantine. Time after time he walked down the pitch, not sideways but frontwards as though out for an afternoon stroll. Constantine dropped short and Gunn stopped the rising ball in front of his nose. The bowler swooped down the pitch, trying to run him out, but each time George blew him a raspberry and scuttled back to safety. We are left to wonder how different the 1921 Test series, during which, in the absence of Hobbs, Gregory and McDonald scythed through the England batting, might have been with Gunn in England's batting line-up. That would not have been the sort of occasion when, in the words of E. V. Lucas' umpire, 'sometimes he would go to sleep'.

Big cricket in the West Indies was not then so sophisticated as it has since become. Spectators, however, were just as excitable and just as noisy. George Gunn did not altogether approve. In the fourth and final Test he was fielding near the sight-screen for Rhodes. Roach, the opening batsman, hit a steeple-high catch into the deep. George stood beneath the dropping ball with his hands in his pockets, quite unconcerned and apparently unaware that a catch was coming. At the last moment he took his right hand out and nonchalantly made the catch one-handed. The others asked him about his casual attitude.

'Oh,' said Gunn, waving an arm round the ground, 'this lot are taking this much too seriously. I thought I'd show them I didn't regard it as being so important.'

On the same tour Patsy Hendren, the game's leading funster, had much amusement from pulling the spectators' legs. Fielding at short leg, for instance, he would crouch down and start creeping towards the batsman and evoke warning shouts of 'Look out, look out, Patsy coming.'

He was a great favourite there, as everywhere else, and his word was widely regarded as gospel. In one Test the West Indies' captain sent a fielder to long leg, but the bowler summoned him to stand closer. He was being shuttled back and forth until he appealed to Patsy, who was batting. 'Skipper tells me go there, bowler says here, where you say I should field, Mr Patsy?'

Patsy told him where he would like him to stand, and there, whatever the skipper and bowler intended, he insisted on staying.

George Gunn's exciting career came to an end in 1932. With Whitsun falling early that year, the traditional match between Nottinghamshire and Surrey at Trent Bridge was only the home team's second of the season. In the first Gunn had taken 67 off the Sussex bowlers, including Tate. Before the start of the

Surrey match he was chatting with the opposing fast bowler, Alf Gover, who asked him how he found batting in first-class cricket at the age of almost 53. Gunn assured him that he managed well enough, except that he did not pick up the short bouncer as quickly. Gover told him not to worry, that he would not be dropping short.

Surrey were a little late into the field. Jardine, the skipper, urged haste. The ball was taken from its greaseproof paper wrapping and thrown straight to Gover, who was given no time to remove the thin grease coating. He ran up to bowl, the ball slipped from his grasp and he sent down a beamer. Gunn did not pick it up and he was struck on the head, from where the ball dropped onto the wicket. Instead of retiring hurt Gunn was out bowled, and out of the game for a long time. Later that season he did play twice more, and had an innings of 74, but the crack on the head so affected him that he did not resume the next season.

So ended the career of a great and fearless batsman, master of improvisation and undoubtedly a cricket law unto himself. Virtually nobody really likes playing fast bowling. I do not know if George Gunn was an exception who did enjoy it; I do know that he relished the challenge. During a match with Lancashire, as I heard from Neville Cardus, the fast bowlers on both sides turned on the heat, McDonald retaliating to Larwood and Voce. The first casualty was Whysall, retired hurt. Soon Nottingham-shire were reeling at 30-odd for 3 with Gunn still at the wicket. He chose the fall of the third wicket to approach McDonald. 'Ted,' he said innocently, 'they told me you were a *fast* bowler.' Magnificent effrontery.

George Gunn and his son G.V. have one distinction, which will surely remain unique. At Edgbaston in 1931 father Gunn made 183 and son Gunn 100 not out. Now that players make their pile and get out early it is doubtful if a father and his son will again even play together in a first-class match.

Playing against the cricketer of fancies, a batting genius for want of a better word, remains among my happiest memories. In the second innings of that 1929 match at Oxford I had

George caught at the wicket. His fancy that day? Obviously to get away quickly.

Gunn and Frank Woolley had much in common. Naturally they had the Golden Age approach to cricket, fitting into a largely professional game played essentially in an amateur spirit and to the spirit of the laws more than to their letter. Woolley was very tall and in ordinary movement languid, looking almost awkward for he seemed to be leaning slightly back as he walked. Once in action he was all flowing grace and elegance, whether batting, bowling or making slip catches.

He was one of the two most difficult batsmen to whom I ever bowled. The other was Spenner Block, cricketer for Cambridge and Surrey, hockey player with 24 England caps and Harlequins rugger player. Block was a very fierce, very straight driver. The bowler either had to drop short of an attacking length, in which case Block's wicket would elude him, or recover very fast in the follow-through to deal with his straight drive. I once opened an innings with him against Sandhurst. His hitting that day was so powerful that, as the non-striking batsman, I kept myself some three yards on the leg-side of the pitch. A slow left-hander and recent Eton and Public Schools captain named Whittaker had a fielder at either end of the sight-screen. Spenner still got a few through to the boundary and scored at a vast pace. We put on upwards of 110 together, I made only 29, and yet Block was out before me.

Woolley was particularly difficult to bowl to because his reach was so great. When he was in the mood there seemed almost nowhere for the bowler to land the ball. The bowler's good length area was greatly reduced. A fraction beyond it and Woolley was hammering the ball off the front foot; a fraction short and it was flying off his bat no less rapidly. He had every scoring stroke recommended in the manual and one or two besides. Among the latter was a hit for six over cover's head, a stroke played off the front foot but one which could not strictly be termed a square cut. In modern times cutting has been done only off the back foot. In those days it was quite common to see the stroke played square off the front foot.

Oxford experienced Woolley's batting in full flow in 1931. We were helpless as he cracked four sixes and twelve fours in an innings of 95. He was often out in the nineties – twice in the 1921 Test at Lord's while Gregory and McDonald were skittling his partners. I hope most of his other dismissals in the nineties were less open to doubt than on that occasion at Oxford. He was lbw to me on an appeal which I checked halfway. He had met everything with the middle of the bat, usually a very forceful bat, so that, when eventually one slipped past and struck his pad, excitement started an appeal. The ball pitched near middle stump and nipped into him, surprisingly and unexpectedly on such a perfect pitch. It would have missed leg stump, as I immediately realised. However, Oxford umpiring was not always too sure and Woolley was given out. He looked disgustedly at the wicket and his pad. Then he walked out to my embarrassment. To reach the pavilion he had to come straight down the pitch. To say 'sorry' would have added insult to injury. I stood in embarrassed silence.

One of those sixes off my bowling was from a hit clean over the pavilion, a truly vast straight drive. Long after the second world war, senior spectators on numerous grounds were still pointing out distant landmarks to which Woolley had dispatched the ball. There was the tree on the high mound on the left side of the Bradford ground, when viewed from the pavilion. Woolley hit Verity to mid-wicket and carried the tree. It was also on that ground that he hit Bowes further than he reckoned he was ever hit by any other batsman. As Bill described it, Woolley had been giving Yorkshire frightful stick and was still on the rampage in the last over before lunch. As Bowes ran up to bowl the last ball Woolley began advancing down the pitch, and he dropped the ball short. Yet Woolley kept on coming and drove on the up, a superb shot such as a brassie would produce on the golf course. The ball was still rising as it cleared the high wall to the left and behind the pavilion.

39

It fell in either the fifth or sixth garden beyond and was not recovered.

Frank's Test career came to an unfortunate end. For long he was an automatic choice against Australia. He was omitted from the 1928–29 touring team under Percy Chapman, but he played in the first two Tests of 1930. In the second he made 41 and 28 as opening batsman in the enforced absence of Sutcliffe. Then in 1934, when such cricket seemed to be just a happy memory for him, he was suddenly recalled for the fifth Test at The Oval. The recall of Rhodes on the same ground eight years earlier had been an inspiration of selection, but that of Woolley was tragedy. He scored four and nought and, when a back injury laid Ames low, he was pressed into service as relief wicket-keeper. The tall, lanky slip-fielder was lost with the gloves on and there were 37 byes.

Selectors take a great chance when they recall a star from the past. The policy fails as often as not. In 1956 Cyril Washbrook, one of the selectors, was brought back to Test cricket after a gap of more than five years. He was in the side against Australia at Headingley. England had lost three wickets for 17 when Washbrook arrived to play an innings of 98 and share a stand of 187 with Peter May. Yet, from a position behind the bowler's arm in the old Headingley press box, I would have given him out lbw when he had made only one. Anti-climax followed, for Washbrook played also in the last two Tests and was dismissed for six and nought.

Woolley's last Test against Australia was a wretched experience, but his last match against the old foe in 1938 was a very different matter. At one time it threatened to be another flop for him. Kent went in against an Australian total of 479, and Woolley ran himself out off the first ball. Kent were skittled for 108 and followed on. The next hour was all Woolley. In that time he hit 81 vintage runs and thrilled us with a six and 13 fours. Woolley still in full flow at the age of 51.

That was his final season and a thoroughly good one, during which his last playing honour was recall to captain the Players against the Gentlemen at Lord's. His side struck trouble in the form of Ken Farnes bowling very fast on a decidedly rough pitch. The innings of the Players started with a ball of fair length from Farnes kicking so sharply that Bill Edrich was knocked out by a blow on the head. When he was revived and preparing to carry on, he was told that he was out; the ball had brushed his glove on its way to his head and had been caught in the gully. Personally, however, Woolley had every reason to be satisfied with his last representative match, for he scored 41 in that uncomfortable first innings and shared the batting honours with Len Hutton. The latter, 29 years his junior, made 52.

Between the wars the pitch at Lord's had its ups and downs. White, the head groundsman, was a forgetful fellow. On one occasion he mislaid his staff's wages, though they were eventually found. On another he allowed a hosepipe to continue running slowly early on the first morning of a Test and part of the pitch was affected. In the 1931 University match I found the metal top of a soft drinks bottle at mid-off. I moved it back some 15 yards, and it was still there when the match ended. A plague of leather-jackets soon afterwards cast a blight on the pitch, which was roundly condemned by the fine Worcestershire bowler, H. A. 'Barmy' Gilbert, as a disgrace and unworthy of the staging of any cricket match. Gilbert was quite a remarkable Golden Age character, who managed without a cricket bag and sometimes arrived at a ground with much of his gear hanging out of his pockets.

I do not remember reference to the famous Lord's ridge between the wars. That seems to have been a post-war treat. It was a curious phenomenon, perhaps still is, for it was not static, nor even uniform in its direction. It appeared in various parts of the square, sometimes nearer one end and sometimes the other. Immediately after the war it made its appearance on the upper side of the ground and its victims were the Public Schools XI. Trevor Bailey, who would have been fast enough for the boys on a true pitch, bowled towards the pavilion end and several times kicked alarmingly from the ridge. He took seven wickets and put the boys out for 104. That was the first year Peter May played at Lord's. He was only 15 at the time. In the first innings Bailey bowled him for a duck, and he did no more than avoid a pair in the second. He may not have made runs, but there was already the stamp of class about his batting. That he failed in such circumstances was not a bad mark against him. Trevor Bailey off that ridge was some proposition. He even laid out his wicket-keeper standing back, who lost sight of the rising ball and was struck on a cheek-bone.

Playing for Oxford and briefly for Surrey, I was able to meet most of the surviving experts from the Golden Age on the field. Two I missed were Jack Hearne – Young Jack – and Patsy Hendren. Middlesex came to The Parks in 1929 but without those two. Not that I would have met them in any case, for it was Barber's policy to give his bowlers occasional breaks and I was rested on that occasion. It is curious how many leading cricketers have not been blessed with robust health. Hearne was one, and though it did not seem to affect him as a county player, his all-round record in Test cricket was unworthy of such a cultured player. His batting was copybook, and his doings with bat and ball in partnership with Frank Tarrant of Australia in the Middlesex team were tremendous. At the age of 21 he began his Test career in Australia in 1911–12 with scores of 76, 43 and 114. Hearne and Tarrant dominated Middlesex cricket in the four years immediately preceding the Great War. They were the major scorers, and they were the major wicket-takers. Hearne's four-season record was 7284 runs, average 45.24, and 432 wickets at 21.7 each. Tarrant made 7031 at 40.4 and took 525 wickets at 17.4.

It was perhaps significant that Hearne's least successful season immediately followed his Australian tour, an indication that he lacked the necessary robust health. Resting in the winter, he then exceeded 2000 runs and 100 wickets in each of the last two peacetime summers. In 1920, the first full post-war season – 1919 was the season of two-day matches with Middlesex playing comparatively little – he repeated the feat.

He never scaled those heights again, though he scored well enough and was usually second to Hendren in the county averages. His leg-break and googly bowling declined more quickly than his batting, and only once subsequently did he reach 100 wickets.

Hearne had outshone Hendren before the war. Afterwards the roles were reversed, for Hendren scaled the batting heights of county and Test cricket. Knowing him well off the field, I should have dearly liked to have played with Patsy. He was a little man, who could have been described as roundly tubby, but that suggests a certain lack of mobility and Patsy was quicksilver in the deep field and close to the wicket alike. He was equally nimble in his footwork as a batsman. His face precisely revealed the man. It was an impish succession of rounded curves, the sort of face artists put on illustrations of Irish leprechauns. He was a man of bubbling humour, an artistic leg-puller, a master at reproducing local accents and a great teller of stories, who could have quickly gained stardom on the music-hall stage.

Shortly before the second world war Patsy and I were given a lift back from a football match by Li Manning, the sports editor of the *Daily Sketch*. Patsy was in top form. He seemed to have some reminiscence for every place we passed. We reached Chiswick Green, and he told us that there he had once made his longest ever hit. 'The ball landed in a fruit cart and finished in Covent Garden,' he related.

The tallest story concerning Patsy had him in two distant places at the same time. His Test career was behind him, but a freelance writer 'sold' him as a Test commentator to a Sunday paper. 'By Patsy Hendren' duly appeared above a piece from Headingley. On the same page a century scored by Hendren E. H. at Old Trafford on the other side of the Pennines was also recorded. Patsy sure was a remarkable man – or two.

The darling of the West Indian spectators was no less popular with Australian crowds, and naturally he was a great attraction everywhere at home. Batsmen of short stature are generally particularly strong on the back foot. They have to be, because they lack the reach of a Woolley in forward play. Patsy was no exception, and there have been few better players of the hook stroke. Yet his quickness of footwork also made him a powerful driver; indeed there were no obvious chinks in his batting armour.

Naturally, Patsy invited opportunities to hook, and Alf Gover tells a story against himself which illustrates that. He was at the start of his career in the Surrey side, and his first encounter with Middlesex was at Lord's. Being young, keen and excited, he was the first member of his side to reach the ground. Only Patsy Hendren was in the professionals' dressing room. He asked Alf who he was and what he did, and his eyes popped when Gover said he was a fast bowler.

'Very fast?' he asked, apparently anxious.

'Oh, yes,' claimed Alf.

'Well,' said Patsy, 'don't forget I'm an old man and don't drop 'em short when I go in.'

Gover took the wicket which brought Patsy to the middle. His eyes lit up and he bowled a bouncer, which Patsy hooked to the Tavern boundary. Muttering 'bloody fluke' to himself, Gover dropped another short, and that time Patsy carried the Tavern boundary for a six. Still not convinced, Alf bowled a third similar ball, and yet again Patsy peppered that boundary: 14 off his first three balls. That was the end of the over, and Jack Hobbs walked across from cover to ask why he was bowling short to Patsy.

'He's afraid of them,' explained Gover.

'Who told you that?'

'He did.'

Hobbs laughed. 'Don't you know he's an Irishman who kisses the Blarney Stone before each season. He's the best hooker in the game.'

His own side was apt to become victims of Patsy's humour. He and Walter Robins were batting together at Lord's. Robins was another quick-footed batsman who often ventured far down the pitch. He was batting at the nursery end on a heavy pitch, when he made one of his charges without making contact. He was so sure he must be stumped that, without looking back, he continued on his way towards the pavilion. A cry of, 'Look out, Skipper,' from Patsy made him turn hurriedly and dive full length for the crease. When he picked himself up, it was to find that he had indeed been well and truly stumped before falling victim to the Middlesex leg-puller. To no avail he had got his pads and trousers covered in mud. Nothing was said when he passed the wicket at the pavilion end on his way out. Patsy had a look of innocent surprise on his face as though to ask what all that was in aid of.

A wonderful, lovable character was Patsy Hendren, with the virtues of those who had enjoyed their cricket education before the Great War. Like the other batsmen of that era he liked to be positive and aggressive from the start. Attack, they were inclined to believe, was often the best means of defence. Les Ames used to talk about a match in which Kent had been set a testing task in rather doubtful pitch conditions. He and Woolley went in together. As they walked to the middle Woolley remarked that the opposing bowlers might be very nasty on that pitch and Ames agreed. 'Right,' said Woolley, 'let's get at them before they can get at us.' Woolley then went straight into the attack. The bowlers were never allowed to settle to exploit the conditions, and Kent cantered home. That was the spirit of the Golden Age.

4
Hobbs on his own

My proudest boast is that I played in the Surrey side with Jack Hobbs. I had admired him from a distance and my earliest memory concerns his fielding. Some time in the early 'twenties I was taken to The Oval, where Surrey were in the field with Jack, of course, at cover. Surrey took an early wicket. Then there was a considerable stand, during which several singles were taken for strokes into the covers. Hobbs seemed unconcerned as he quietly fielded and tossed the ball back to Strudwick behind the stumps or to the bowler. Suddenly Hobbs erupted. He was on the move and accelerating as the stroke was played. Again the batsmen ran, and one of them was out by a couple of yards when Jack's throw dropped the ball into Struddy's gloves just above the stumps.

During the 1911–12 tour of Australia, Hobbs ran out 15 opponents, an average of exactly one a match. He was an artist in that position. Not for him the modern practice of hurling the ball as hard as possible to the stumper whether the batsmen are running or not. Like the bowlers of his time, Jack was ready to trade runs for wickets. He lured opponents to destruction by allowing them to think they could run with impunity for strokes gently directed towards cover. Even those who knew Jack's cricket well were taken in.

It is a pity that run-out records have not been kept. Hobbs would surely head the list with much to spare. He must have spent around 1300 innings in the field, and although he certainly did not maintain that fantastic average of a run-out per match, the total would still be formidable if he averaged one in three matches; his 1300 innings would mean 800 to 900 matches with upwards of 250 run-outs.

Plum Warner was the official captain of the 1911–12 side, but illness prevented him playing after he had made 151 in the opening match against South Australia. He was thus a spectator, while Johnny Douglas led his side. After the tour he wrote of Hobbs in *Wisden*:

> Not even G. L. Jessop at his best is his superior. Wonderfully quick in moving to the ball, neat with his feet, and with a pair of hands which were not only always in the right place but which seemed to act as a magnet to the ball, Hobbs has a beautiful and fast return. I have never seen a cover point hit the wicket so often, his underarm throw-in being particularly deadly in this respect.

There have been numerous famous fielders at cover since, men who saved many, many runs. None have been such valuable tacticians and contributed so much to their side's success as Hobbs. We have had Bland of South Africa, very quick and with a deadly throw, and Clive Lloyd in the same mould. Today, Derek Randall and David Gower shine brilliantly at cover, and both have brought off dazzling run-outs. They are, of course, helped by the conditions of modern county play. Running judgment has been sadly eroded by the requirements of limited-overs cricket. It is not easy for a batsman to adjust to the needs of serious cricket after joy-riding in the one-day nonsense. What I have against the modern fielder is his habit of revealing his throwing power the first time the ball comes to him. The first cover fielder I saw who gave himself away by blazing at the stumps at the first opportunity was Jack Davies in the Kent side. He had a very powerful throw and very soon everyone on the ground knew it, including the batsmen who acted accordingly.

Surrey thought to improve the throwing of their side by inviting an American baseball pitcher to instruct their fielders at The Oval before one season. The session ended with the base-baller accepting a lesson from Jack. Hobbs is remembered as batsman and fielder. Those who knew him in his early days assert that he could also have become a high-ranking medium-pace bowler. In 1920 he did indeed head the listed bowling averages with 17 wickets at 11.82 each. Second with 161 wickets was Rhodes, his old batting partner.

In 1926 I was introduced to Test cricket by one of the greatest innings Hobbs ever played. That was the occasion when England won the Ashes for the first time since 1912. Hobbs and Sutcliffe played through an Oval sticky in an opening stand of 172, and Jack made exactly 100. I can still visualise his hundredth run. He played a ball from Jack Gregory with such delicacy that for a few strides Hobbs and the ball seemed to be moving together. In fact, the ball slanted out towards Andrews, one of Australia's finest fielders, who was at very short extra cover. Andrews never managed a shy at either wicket. Sutcliffe was on the move as Hobbs played the stroke, and by the time Andrews reached the slowly trickling ball he was sliding his bat safely across the batting crease. Andrews had to turn to throw at the far wicket, and Hobbs had ample time to trot home without ever breaking into a sprint.

Long after the event there has been debate about the bowling of Arthur Richardson. Richardson was a tall, heavily built man able to get lift from a sticky pitch. For nearly an hour Richardson bowled his off-breaks, supported by a tight leg-side field, almost exclusively to Hobbs. He was bowling round the wicket, aiming to pitch around off stump and turn the ball into the batsman. He was getting both turn and lift, and for ten overs while the pitch was most spiteful, runs were very scarce at that end. I recall Hobbs scoring a single, and that was all. The other nine overs were maidens, of which Hobbs played eight.

It has been suggested that Hobbs was bluffing to keep the bespectacled Arthur Richardson on and other spinners off.

Debate has perhaps been sparked off by a comment in the *Wisden* report that 'he would probably have been deadly had he bowled over the wicket with something like a normally placed field'. Only the writer knew what he meant by 'a normally placed field', for in those conditions Richardson's tactics and field placing were precisely what George Macaulay employed. And Macaulay went through sides on stickies as quickly as any left-handed spinner, including Arthur Mitchell's match at Old Trafford, when he far outpaced Verity. All off-spinners of that and subsequent periods, including Jupp, Tom Goddard, Johnny Clay, Jim Laker and Fred Titmus, used the same tactics. Moreover, what the writer in *Wisden* overlooked was that Richardson did bowl over the wicket in the first two overs of that spell, and they cost 11 runs. From there he turned the ball far too much and eliminated the chance of lbw. Hobbs hit him for two fours to leg in his first over.

I am quite sure that Hobbs was not bluffing, although he was never other than complete master of his fate. He played Richardson as surely as he played the other spinners on that spiteful turf. Sutcliffe had his adventures and was at times beaten; Hobbs never was. Furthermore, if Richardson was not the menace which the course of the play and the sight of his kicking deliveries suggested, Hobbs would not have stayed opposite him so much. He was the number one of the partnership, accustomed to go to the point of most danger. That he so appropriated Richardson's bowling and left Sutcliffe mainly at the opposite end indicated where the real danger lay. That Richardson was the likeliest to break through is apparent when the other spinners are considered. Two of them were leg-break and googly bowlers, Arthur Mailey and Clarrie Grimmett. When a pitch is sticky, such top-spinning bowlers do not get the venomous lift which orthodox spinners do. The other slow bowler on that occasion was Charles Macartney, the left-hander, whose best bowling days were in the past. Indeed, in post-war Test cricket he took just four wickets against England and seven against South Africa.

Four years later, on the same ground, Jack's brilliant Test career ended. He was then approaching 48. As he came to play his last innings, accompanied by Sutcliffe, he was tremendously received by the great crowd. In the middle, before he took guard, all the Australian fielders gathered round to give him three cheers. In such an emotionally charged atmosphere it was not surprising that he made only 9. Even so he did better than Don Bradman 18 years later. The Don also was playing his final Test match innings. He was given the same rapturous welcome by the spectators and treated to three cheers by the English players. He was promptly bowled by Eric Hollies for a duck, which reduced his overall Test average to just under 100.

Hobbs remained the master player right to the end. His last season was 1934, when he was gently easing himself out of the county game. A total of 624 in 15 completed innings, which included a final century against Lancashire – that season's champions – did not suggest serious decline. A few seasons earlier, when he was already a veteran, he was still charming opponents with his technique. Jack Iddon, a newcomer to the Lancashire side, was fielding mid-off to Ted McDonald's bowling when Hobbs played the ball straight at him. Iddon let the ball through his legs and Hobbs scored two. McDonald was not amused, and Iddon apologised. 'I'm sorry about that,' he said when he returned from chasing the ball. 'I was so engrossed watching his footwork that I took my eye off the ball.'

Nigel Haig, a contemporary of Jack who captained Middlesex at their most difficult time of bowling weakness between the wars, once asked him how he himself rated his own batting.

'I think I was a pretty good player before the war. Afterwards my batting was rather straightforward,' Hobbs replied modestly.

It was during the 'afterwards' that my generation, including Iddon, were captivated by the magic of his cricket. He was 36 when that war ended, already approaching the veteran stage for most players. Yet he made rather more than two-thirds of his 197 first-class centuries subsequently. He was in his forty-third year when he made 16 centuries in 1925. Twice that summer he hit a century in each innings of a match, including the Taunton game with Somerset when he left W. G. Grace's record 126 hundreds behind. Such was his record immediately before and in the years following the Great War, a succession of triumphs, it is reasonable to estimate that the four lost years, 1915–18, cost him 12,000 runs and 50 centuries. He missed four home seasons and two overseas tours. The estimate is on the conservative side.

It was in July 1931 that I played alongside Jack Hobbs, literally alongside, for he fielded cover and I started at extra cover. The bowler was Alf Gover, who was quite as fast as any England bowler of the 'seventies and early 'eighties. He had an extra cover and a mid-off, which may surprise all who have now become accustomed to opening pace-bowlers operating with just one off-side fielder in front of the wicket. The difference is explained by the fact that the modern bowler partly wastes the new ball by pitching short and virtually eliminating forward play. A bowler such as Gover had a full complement of fielders behind and in front of the wicket on the off-side. Nobody can attack on both sides of the wicket at the same time, for he does not have enough fielders to cover both sides. That is as true now as it ever was, but the modern seeks to cover both sides – the absurd split field – and pitches short defensively. The opening bowlers of the Hobbs era bowled to a full attacking length, luring the opponent forward. In that same month I spent some time fielding third slip to Gover. I was anxious and apprehensive. Gover used to bowl several half-volleys swinging away. Any batsman driving and edging would give a very fast-moving catch in the region of third slip.

On that, my first outing, Gover lost no time in taking the first Worcestershire wicket, and Hobbs walked across to talk to me. That was the nicest thing that ever happened to me on the cricket field. The newcomer could have had no personal interest for Jack. He came across to make a nervous young amateur feel at home in the side. Hobbs was more than a great cricketer; he was a great man. In general I disapprove of the award of knighthoods for games players, but I would always make an exception of Hobbs. He carried the title Sir John Hobbs worthily and modestly.

He himself may have dismissed his post-war batting as rather straightforward. It did not seem that way to opponents. Jack Mercer, a splendid opening bowler who played for Sussex, Glamorgan and Northamptonshire, could testify to that. Northamptonshire were due to meet Surrey, and they discussed how they might rid themselves of Hobbs at reasonable cost. It was decided to try to run him out at the outset, exploiting his known liking for tapping the ball on the off-side and getting off the mark with a single. The plot was hatched but came sadly to grief.

'I bowled just the ball we needed, pitching in the right place swinging away, but Jack might have known what was intended,' Mercer explained afterwards. 'Instead of tapping it towards the fast-approaching cover fielder he hit it to the square-leg boundary! How he did it I don't know.' Definitely a stroke devised and perfected in the days before 1915, but not one for ordinary mortals to borrow.

With Sandham in the Surrey side and Sutcliffe for England, Jack had perfect understanding between wickets. It must have been the same pre-war when his partners were Tom Hayward and Rhodes. So good was the understanding that there was seldom need to call. Intuition guided them, and the sharp single brought them hundreds of runs. The secret of taking sharp singles towards cover lies in the striker making up his mind about running as he strikes the ball. The batsman backing up from the far end can then break into top speed at once. Any hesitation and the non-striker has to check, lose momentum and be unable to reach the far end in safety.

Others were not always so adept at running. Against Kent at The Oval in that 1931 season, Percy Fender was run out off the first ball of our second innings. We needed 204 in rather less than two hours. Fender decided to go for the runs although rain had affected the pitch. If anyone should have known Hobbs, he was the Surrey captain. Yet when Hobbs called for a single off the first ball Fender was caught flat-footed. That summarily ended our dash for victory. Percy George, his moustache bristling, sent the dressing room attendant, former Surrey batsman Goatly, to tell the professionals that we were reverting to the original order. That meant that I dropped back from no. 5 to no. 8, and in the event I had to play for a draw with Bob Gregory through the final 25 minutes, knowing that Ted Sheffield, the other opening bowler, was absent ill.

Like many, many others I claim that Jack Hobbs was the greatest batsman. He was the master on all types of pitch, his technique developed to overcome any difficulties. His superiority over Bradman stems from their difference in the wet. The Don did not consider that cricket should be played other than on a dry pitch, and apparently he made no attempt to master the art of wet-pitch batting. Indeed, he cut a very sorry figure on occasions when the pitch was sticky, including the 1934 Test at Lord's, where Verity took 14 wickets on the third day. Bradman had fallen to Verity in the dry on the Saturday evening for 36. On the wet in the second innings he played the most unworthy stroke, a swipe which would not have pleased a tail-ender, and skied a simple catch for stumper Ames to take.

On the dry there was no question that Bradman was the number one. Yet, when measuring his triumphs against those of Hobbs, we must remember the changed circumstances. Hobbs began playing big cricket when Tests in England lasted only three days. The game was geared accordingly. By the time Bradman came on the scene they were played over four days here and, of course, to a finish in his own country. Bradman proceeded to make the four-day game obsolete as he ground out the runs through the first, the second and the third century. The concept of what the side needed was utterly changed.

I remember the debate following England's defeat at Lord's in 1930, when the Don hammered 254 in 330 minutes. On the first day England had made 405 for 9. Duleepsinhji in his first Test against Australia had brilliantly hit 173 and recklessly lost his wicket to a deep-field catch near the close. In the post-mortem he was taken to task, not least by his uncle Ranjitsinhji, but the chief conclusion concerned the timing of the English innings. It was said that there was nothing much wrong with the final total of 425, but the innings ended too soon. The side batting first in a four-day match needed to play through until lunch on the second day. Of course, it was unheard of previously in England for a side making 800 runs to be beaten. Australia did indeed win with time to spare. However, such was the positive tempo of cricket then that 508 overs were bowled. Four days and 508 overs in a Test in 1930; five days and 350 overs – if the spectators were lucky – in a Test between India and England in the winter of 1981–82.

Bradman was mainly responsible for changing the concept of Test cricket. He was the scoring machine of perfectly oiled parts turning out runs galore. Hobbs played at a time when it was necessary to get on with the scoring job, get out and get the other side out. If Hobbs had been an exact contemporary of the Don, and hence differently schooled in the playing of cricket, might he not have been an equally remorseless accumulator of runs? None can say, but I do affirm that, because of his greater versatility, Jack was a greater batsman than the Don.

Press photography in the years before the Great War was still in its infancy. Most of the alleged action pictures were not taken from actual play but were posed, and thoroughly deceptive most of them were. In 1963 *Wisden* reproduced a picture which carried the caption: 'Jack Hobbs, the dashing batsman, when he delighted his admirers before the first world war.' If his admirers had seen him playing like that, they would have swooned. This was a posed picture taken quite obviously on the nursery at Lord's. It shows Jack prancing out to slog, and I write slog advisedly. He has both elbows above the shoulders, the right sticking out at such an angle that the wrist must have been locked. From that position he could only have scooped, and the position of body and legs is most unnatural for a cultured batsman.

It is a curious fact that, when asked to pose for a particular picture, the great player often has not the foggiest idea how he actually does play his strokes – nor how he bowled. It is left to lesser mortals like me to analyse cricket techniques. The great do not need to. Unfortunately, therefore, the many posed pictures of those players leave to posterity a totally erroneous impression. No true batsman, big hitters included, have ever lifted both elbows above the shoulders in the pick-up, nor have they ever jumped or pranced down the pitch. When moving out they glide, left foot towards the line of the ball with right foot advancing behind the left and so on. Believe me, Jack never played such an undisciplined stroke as that published by *Wisden* in 1963.

There are many absurd so-called 'action' pictures of great bowlers also taken on the nursery at Lord's. There is a shocker of Victor Trumper leaping out to drive and an even worse one of Ranjitsinhji leaping. His arms and bat are high above the shoulders, and his left foot in the prance is about 18 inches off the ground. One day at Oxford a press photographer asked Pataudi – the first cricketing Pataudi – to pose for an action picture 'jumping' out to drive. Pat remembered the freakish picture of Ranji. He imitated it precisely, and that monstrosity also saw the light of day in the papers.

Beware posed action pictures, which give such a wrong impression of the great players of the past. Bradman was more fortunate. Photography had so advanced that his action pictures were taken in actuality and accurately show how he played.

5

Bradman the single-minded

Except that they both had exceptional cricketing ability, Hobbs and Bradman were poles apart. Throughout his time Hobbs was at peace with all; Bradman in his early years in big cricket seemed to be at war with several of those around him. That was not necessarily something for which he was to blame, certainly not exclusively. He had to take some ribbing when he first went to Sydney as a raw country lad from Bowral in New South Wales. He was not versed in the ways of a big city, and his clothing for nets on the Sydney Cricket Ground was unorthodox. His trousers, it was reported, were supported by a pair of braces. One way and another he had a rough start in the state's capital city, and it seemed to turn him against people.

The Don did not get on with several of his playing colleagues, and on tour in England there was dispute about the agreed sharing of extra-mural gains. There was, too, the Australian antipathy between Protestants and Roman Catholics. This was something novel and difficult to understand when I first toured Australia in 1946–47. The two religious groups at that time kept very much apart, except Lindsay Hassett, who was often to be found at Protestant parties. At that time Liberal supporters even attributed the success of the Labour Party in the country's first

56

post-war election to the Roman Catholics having been ordered to vote that way by their priests. It was never so noticeable subsequently, but to the end the Roman Catholics in the Australian team were very decidedly anti-Bradman. It is probable that his unpopularity in certain quarters was because he was not understood. Perhaps only his charming wife, Jennie, really understood him.

During his playing days he did not have much time for the press. Later, when he was the top cricket administrator at the Adelaide Oval, he treated the writers splendidly. It seemed that he had shed the tensions of his active career and was an excellent boss of South Australian cricket. He even joined the press to write for the *Daily Mail* during the 1953 and 1956 Australian tours of England. Advised by Alex Bannister, his closest friend among the journalists, he did a fine commentating job, particularly during the first of the two ventures.

I never played cricket with the Don, but I did play golf with him and that gave a clue to his make-up. During tours the English players and press used to have a Christmas Day golf competition among themselves in the afternoon. In 1965 we were spending Christmas in Adelaide and Bradman was invited to join us. It was a light-hearted affair, a Stableford four-ball competition. Bradman's partner was Denis Compton.

About the seventh hole Denis lost a ball and walked on. Just after the turn Bradman played an apparently perfect second shot with wood at a long hole, but the ball ran off the right side of the green. It must have been close and the rough there was short. Yet we could not find it. In such a light-hearted affair I cannot imagine anyone except the Don going back well over 200 yards to play a second ball. He did, losing stroke and distance, which meant that he was playing four. That time the ball finished on the green and two putts gave him a six, which meant he salvaged a point. Playing off handicap 1, he played that round with the utmost seriousness and overcame the championship Kooyonga course, one of the best I ever played, with a gross score of 71, despite the loss of those two shots. He was, of course, the winner.

To the Don the least important event had considerable significance. He was incapable of not taking it very seriously. He strove to do well in that trivial Christmas afternoon outing as though playing in a Test match. That power of perpetual concentration explains his phenomenal cricketing success, his lofty class as a golfer and his success in business starting from scratch. I am quite sure he could have succeeded at anything, because once started he would have put the whole of himself into it. He was one of the two most remarkable people I ever met. The other was a charming and amusing American who, as a divorcee, married into an aristocratic French family. Taking bishops and cardinal in her stride, she overcame the opposition of the Roman Catholic Church to obtain special dispensation. She similarly proved too good for the shocked French family, headed by the Comte, and kept her fiancé, who was anxious about opposing Church and family, up to the mark. Later she took on the Nazis when they arrived at their château in La Vendée, flying the Stars and Stripes and resisting attempts at requisition. She failed only to secure the release of her husband who had become a prisoner-of-war, although, wheedling petrol from the Germans, she pursued her cause to Paris and then all the way to the frontier across which he had just been taken. Finally she climbed the Pyrenees with her infant daughter to get away from the Nazis. Don Bradman and Greta Perreau de Launay had much in common.

On the cricket field Bradman was the complete fielder and, in dry conditions, the complete batsman. Years after he retired I saw a film showing him playing all the strokes. What struck me was how late he seemed to play the stroke and yet how much time he had for its playing. The answer lay in the speed and exactness of his footwork. The camera can reveal much that the eye misses. After seeing that, I could understand more how he was able to hook Maurice Tate during that 254 at Lord's in 1930. Tate had a fielder deep on the leg-side in front of the old

Tavern. He began with him square and Bradman directed the hook between mid-wicket and mid-on. The fielder was moved towards the old clock-tower, and Bradman's next hook directed the ball square to the Tavern. The Don could not have had much time to spare making the stroke. Tate was hasty off the pitch, and he did not bowl long hops. Bradman with that perfect footwork was able to hook balls just short of a length – the sort that are now bowled so much for defensive purposes. His hooking of Tate remains my main memory of that magnificent innings.

Strangely, I found a certain boredom creeping into watching him churn out the runs; not because his strokeplay was ever less than exhilarating, but because there was such inevitability about his innings. If Bradman was not dismissed very early, it became quickly apparent that nothing was likely to shift him. This was borne out by that 1930 Test at Lord's. Two tremendous catches by Percy Chapman, one when he was sated with runs and the other when he had made only one in the second innings, dismissed him. Chapman picked up the first at short extra cover with his right hand close to the turf, a very hard-hit chance. The second in the gully was another low, one-handed effort when the ball was cut fiercely off Tate.

That summer Bradman was 21 and at his most dashing. His scoring rate was anything between 40 and 60 an hour. It was seldom as low as the first figure, and he approached the second when he made 309 in a single day at Headingley. Again four years later he topped 300 on that same ground, but on both occasions rain helped England to escape the consequences of his vast and very rapid scoring. Although the resolute Leyland was still batting, England were facing defeat by an innings in 1934, when the floods came late on the last morning. They were still 155 behind with six second innings wickets down, but very soon the low-lying area in front of the old pavilion was a vast lake, and that was that.

The only bowler to puzzle Bradman during his first tour was an amateur of his own age, Ian Peebles, who was brought in for the last two Tests. At Old Trafford his leg-breaks and googlies did have the great man guessing once or twice, and he fell to Peebles for 14. That was the only Test in which he did not make a large score. His Test average was 139 from a record total of 974, and in all first-class matches, in which he was just short of 3000, it was 98.7.

Bradman added to his cricketing fame when he also revealed his ability as a skipper. He led Australia in the last series before the war and the first afterwards. On both occasions he was opposed by Walter Hammond, who was among those who did not like Bradman. It did not make for harmonious relations in 1946–47 in Australia. That was unfortunate, for between the two Test series there had been a splendid Victory series in 1945 between sides representing England and the Australian Services then in Britain. Hammond led England's sides and Lindsay Hassett was the Australian captain. Lindsay was one of cricket's smallest men, but he was big of heart and brimful of fun and humour. That was a series of unsullied good humour and much splendidly entertaining cricket. Only two of the Services players went on to represent Australia, Hassett and Keith Miller, but Ces Pepper, leg-break and googly bowler and powerful batsman, would surely have been a third if he had stayed in Australia instead of migrating to Lancashire to play League cricket.

Hassett could well have become captain earlier than he did, for Bradman had been seriously ill and it was doubtful if he would play in 1946. The Don tried himself out against Hammond's bowlers for South Australia. Without his usual domination and at the pedestrian rate of 30 an hour, he made 76 and 3. He was chosen for the first Test in Brisbane, but it was still not certain that he would play through the series. If he had been given out when he was first out, that would almost certainly have been his final Test. He batted thoroughly badly while scoring his first 28, and the edge of his bat was given unusually hard work. Then he slapped at Bill Voce, edged again, and Jack Ikin took a shoulder-high catch at second slip. Bradman stayed, and the umpire on appeal allowed him to continue.

Bradman thought he had played the ball onto the ground and thence to second slip. That was quite impossible. He played a cross-batted slap outside the off stump. To be a bump ball it would need to have made contact with the under edge of that slanting bat. In that event the ball would have gone towards fine leg, perhaps hitting the wicket on the way. The only way that ball could possibly have reached second slip shoulder-high was off the upper edge, and it could not then have made contact with the ground.

That rather set the tone for the series, in which the enmity of the two skippers played an important part. After being granted a second innings Bradman suddenly became himself and, sharing a stand of 276 with Hassett, he made 187 to ensure his playing in the next nine Tests against England. The umpiring of Scott and Borwick was consistently against England. There were two more glaring errors. In Melbourne Bill Edrich, who seemed set to complete a second successive Test century, was given out lbw when he had played the ball. In Adelaide Cyril Washbrook was sent packing to a first bounce catch by Tallon behind the stumps. Tallon did not appeal and said he had not made a catch, but Washbrook had to go. Those were the worst, but there were others, and in the fourth Test a magic-eye camera series in a Melbourne paper showed that Bradman had been plumb lbw to Doug Wright and reprieved.

It was a curious fact that the worst umpiring against England in Australia occurred during series in which they had no chance of winning. Bradman's side was much too strong in all departments for an English side fatally short of bowling, and in 1958–59, the chucking season, Australia would have romped home without the aid of umpires.

To the end Bradman remained a great batsman, but his most brilliant innings were played at breakneck speed during his early Test years. When he came to England in 1938 he was still scoring heavily but not so quickly, and on his fourth and last visit as a player in 1948 his scoring pace was that of ordinary mortals. Modern spectators may wonder at his great rate of scoring, but it must be remembered that the tempo of Test cricket was double what it was in the sad winter of 1981–82. When Bradman hit his 254 in 5½ hours at Lord's, he was receiving just over 23 overs an hour. Nevertheless, even at the old brisk tempo the Don was unusually fast, thanks to the versatility of his stroke play.

Nearly four years after he retired the South Africans on tour went to Adelaide. They were instructed one day to go to the ground very early. On arrival they found Bradman changed, padded and armed to give them a demonstration of batting. Jackie McGlew wrote about it in his autobiography. The South Africans were amazed at the range of his strokes. As McGlew said, one ball would be struck in the general direction of mid-off, while its exact reproduction a few deliveries later would be hammered wide of mid-on. McGlew claimed that he was the only bowler who got the ball past Bradman's bat, and that only because it hit the side netting on its way!

In 20 years of Test cricket his average dropped below 65 in only one series. That was in 1932–33, the season of England's fast leg-theory bowling, which in itself was a great compliment to his batting, for it was specially planned to curb his scoring. For anyone else an average of 56.57 would have been cause for delight. In Bradman's case it indicated that he had been curbed, but still not mastered. He was never mastered in dry conditions in which, however spitefully the ball might turn, he matched the skill of Hobbs. On a consistently spiteful pitch in Melbourne in 1932–33 he followed a first innings duck, victim to the first ball of Bill Bowes, with a score of 103 not out. The Australian total was only 191, and Bradman made his runs out of 164. Only once in that game did a side top 200, and for the only time in that series England were the losers.

As good as any of his mammoth scores was his 103 in 1938 at Headingley, where in four Test visits he never failed to reach three figures. That was a spin-bowler's benefit match from start to finish, a thriller all through and undoubtedly one of the greatest Tests, and a much closer affair than the five-wickets margin in favour of Australia suggests. While 35 wickets were falling only 695 runs were made, and the top scorer on each side was the top batsman. Bradman made his century and Hammond 76, which I suppose roughly reflected their respective merit. If Bradman could master the awkwardly turning ball on the dry, we cannot doubt that he could have mastered it in the wet, if he had not had that peculiar quirk in his make-up which persuaded him that cricket in the wet was not cricket.

6
Survivors of the Golden Age

With Surrey my experience against the 1914 survivors was extended to embrace two batsmen, Ernest Tyldesley and Phil Mead, and all-rounders George Brown and Alec Kennedy. As a left-hander Mead was the opposite of Woolley; where the latter was flashing he was stolidly circumspect. There was nothing graceful about his batting, but it was splendidly organised and very effective. He looked massive at the wicket, as he tugged at his cap and tapped his left thigh with the fingers of his left hand before each ball, and occasionally twiddled his bat. His bat also looked massively broad to the bowler trying to find a way round his solid defence. The Yorkshire bowlers reckoned that he was the best judge of what to play and what he could ignore near the off stump. Frequently Mead would play no stroke, the bowler would anticipate success, and the ball would narrowly miss the wicket.

Mead was another leading batsman overlooked in that season of crazy selection in 1921 until the final two Tests, by which time the series had already been lost. Then he hit the highest score that had yet been made for England at home. His 17 Tests – average nearly 50 – were widely spaced. He toured Australia twice with a gap of 17 years, and, when he arrived for the second time in 1928, he was greeted by an ancient with, 'I remember your father playing here in 1911.' It is customary to think of Mead as dour. In fact, in addition to his sure defence, he had strokes to score in all directions. Whereas Woolley's lovely strokes were conspicuous, Mead's, punched rather than stroked, tended to slip through without causing a stir. Yet the runs came well enough. His 182 unfinished in the Oval Test in 1921 were scored at a rate of 36 an hour off Gregory, McDonald, Mailey and Armstrong.

It was at that same Dean Park, where I first discovered that cricket was a serious undertaking and not just a pastime for boys, that 12 years later I fielded while Mead made one of his 153 centuries. We fielded also through 47 runs by George Brown, who was another George Gunn in his eccentricities. Every time there was a bump ball, taken first bounce by a fielder, some in the crowd jumped to the conclusion that he was out. Brown invariably played up to them by walking away as though he was going out. That is more acceptable to spectators than to fielders, who are apt to find the repetition rather tiring.

Brown was one of the strongest men who ever played cricket. He was tall and broad and had large hands. In the cricketing line he did everything. He was a dashing left-handed batsman; he put those great hands to splendid use at mid-off, where they closed on the hardest hit; despite his size he was a stumper good enough for England; and he was a tearaway fast right-handed bowler. A veritable one-man band. Indeed, when England were doing so badly in the 1921 Tests, a humorous cartoonist suggested that Brown should bowl from one end, dash down the pitch while the ball was in flight and don the gloves at the other. Another cartoonist in *The Cricketer* depicted the England openers venturing forth to meet Gregory and McDonald, the one in a suit of armour, the other in a Michelin tyre suit. Prophecy indeed, for nearly half a century later came motor-cycling helmets and other defensive gear to cover batting weakness.

Brown, like the other remarkable George, was prone to make

odd gestures. There was the occasion when he deliberately breasted away a fast-rising ball from McDonald for four leg-byes. In his book, *Three Straight Sticks*, Bob Wyatt relates how Brown batted with a chunk of bat. He and Lionel Tennyson had had words, and the latter relegated him to no. 10. Brown, still angry, arrived at the wicket with an ancient relic of a bat which he had picked up in the pavilion. Soon the old weapon split, Brown tore off the loose piece and continued batting successfully with the remains.

If Patsy Hendren was the master at reproducing local dialects and accents, Brown was just as accomplished at imitating animal sounds. At Worcester on one occasion he played a dog. At that time, the old pavilion being very small, the players used to have meals in a marquee. Brown, barking fiercely, entered beneath the tent's flap and with his powerful claw he grasped Maurice Jewell, the Worcestershire captain, by a heel. Jewell leaped to his feet, sending the trestle table flying and all the provender with it. The incident did not go down well with the Worcestershire skipper. Not, I imagine, that Brown was a whit disturbed, for he was quite incorrigible. On tour in India, the team took part in a big game shoot while staying with a maharajah. At the end of the day the trophies were laid out on the lawn with labels to indicate the marksmen responsible. Next morning it was discovered that all the prize specimens were labelled George Brown. The muddled trophies defied unscrambling.

Brown also was brought into the 1921 Test side as batsman-stumper. In the last three matches he made 250 in five innings, and in the last two he was Jack Russell's opening partner. The same risky experiment of dropping the best wicket-keeper to accommodate one who was also a fine batsman was taken before the historic Oval Test of 1926. Brown was again chosen in place of Strudwick, but injury kept him out of the match and Struddy resumed his rightful place.

After his playing days George Brown became an umpire and surely the worst ever. He had a twitching finger, and up it went in answer to almost every appeal. It was said that he was the only umpire who ever completed his 100 in May. He lasted only one season. He was then dropped, to his utter astonishment, for, despite grumbling by his many victims, he was convinced that he had done a good job. He was so convinced that he requested and obtained an interview on the subject with Billy Findlay, the MCC secretary. The last heard of Brown the umpire was while he was coaching at Sandhurst. There, on a reprehensible appeal, he gave an unfortunate out when the ball was missing the leg stump by inches. 'And that's to teach you to play it with the bat,' George announced.

Rather earlier, in fact before the start of the first season after the second world war, Hampshire had a practice match. George was allowed to officiate. He regarded the game largely as a coaching session, for he kept holding up the play while he instructed players in the error of their ways. Among those who 'benefited' was Desmond Eagar, the new Hampshire captain and secretary who had played for Gloucestershire before the war. After that experience the Hampshire chairman told Eagar that, while George would always be very welcome on the ground, 'he must never be allowed to umpire again'.

A third player in that Hampshire side who had made his mark before the Great War was Alec Kennedy. He was then aged 40 but still bowling fast-medium and still very lively off the pitch. He ended my Surrey hopes. I never expected to do much with the ball, for, having concentrated entirely throughout the season on helping to overcome Cambridge, I knew in the anti-climax that I was stale. I did, however, hope to do something with the bat, and the chance came at Bournemouth. I managed to persuade Fender to allow me to be night-watchman, reckoning that Giles Baring, the Hampshire fast bowler, might dismiss Tom Barling early. There was a brief discussion, for Douglas Jardine opposed the move. I had made 60-odd in a match when Jardine was in the opposition, and now he paid me a great compliment by suggesting that I was too good with the bat to be thrown away as a night-watchman.

However, Barling did succumb to Baring and I went in. I

stayed to the close and was getting going well enough the next morning. I had scored nine when Kennedy sent down one of full length. One of my superstitions was that 13 was my lucky batting number. The message reached my mind that here was the magic 13 for the asking as I launched a straight drive. I suppose I fell between two stools, whether to loft it over Kennedy's head or to hug the turf. In the event it flew very fast straight for his left knee. He made an instinctive thrust of his left hand while ducking the knee, and the ball stuck for a splendid catch.

Midway between the wars not many bowlers of pre-war vintage could be expected to be still going strong in the first-class game. In fact, there were several spinners and here and there a long-lasting bowler of quicker pace, the best of whom were Kennedy, Nigel Haig and George Geary, who played in the epic 1926 Test, plus Tate who switched from bowling slows.

Kennedy played just one series for England, in which he headed the bowlers by taking 31 South African wickets for under 20 runs each in 1922–23. Although he had the competition of Cecil Parkin in the early post-war years and then Tate, Kennedy might have qualified for more Tests if he and Jack Newman had not been so heavily worked in the Hampshire side. They were Hampshire bowling for many years, and they were also required to do so much batting that each completed the double five times. Together they accounted for nearly 5000 first-class wickets.

When I first saw Kennedy in 1919 – Newman had not yet returned from war service – he had a long run and a habit of crossing his forearms in front of his chest just before going into the delivery stride. It looked most attractive, but soon he modified his method, cut out the arm crossing and reduced the length of his run. The new action was beautifully rhythmic and enabled him to keep taking county wickets until he finally retired at 45.

Newman I knew and appreciated greatly only after he had retired. He was another whose health was not robust, and he retired ultimately to South Africa. Given good health, he could well have gone further than Kennedy, for he had a very good off-break bowled at brisk pace and the heart to keep plugging away. His normal pace was medium-quick. He was four years older than Kennedy, but despite his frail health he also kept going into his forties. It seems fantastic that he should have done his last double when he was 41. He almost did so again the next year, 1929, but there his career abruptly ended. Physical troubles prevented him from playing at all in the following season.

The partnership was formed in the early years of the century, and for 11 years from 1920 they continued in harness. During that time they completed their doubles and, averaging just on 2000 overs a season, they accounted for 2911 wickets. It was an exceptionally long alliance by two men bowling at their pace and also making so many runs. Certainly in the past 100 years their joint record of long service as pace-bowlers is unique.

When I played against Geary in 1931 he was past his best. He lives in my memory mainly as one of a string of defensive bowlers of medium pace and upwards, who made playing against Leicestershire a dull business. Of that particular match *Wisden* recorded that 'Wellings not only punished the Leicestershire bowling with some freedom . . .' It was very mild punishment, for after hitting a four over mid-off I could play forward subsequently only while Astill was briefly bowling his off-breaks. An hour was spent making 32, and none should apply the word freedom to that rate. The string of negative bowlers was Shipman, Coleman, Snary and Geary. Neville Cardus once expressed the view that the true Golden Age was the 'thirties. Looking back he must have remembered Bradman and Hammond and the scintillating seasons of 1938 and 1939, and have forgotten that we had quite an amount of dull cricket earlier in the decade.

The true Golden Age took in Grace's last Test appearance, brought out Hobbs, and was graced by Victor Trumper and the greatest bowler of the modern game, Sydney Barnes. Barnes was 62 when I played with him in 1938 as members of a press team captained by Douglas Jardine. For two overs I stood at first slip for his bowling. In the third Jardine came to the slips and said 'Move over; I want to watch him too.' That afternoon Barnes took seven wickets for about 35 runs. He was now slow-medium, but his action was still packed with spring and rhythm, and he still moved the ball a little this way and then a little that way. Neither of his two slips could see any difference in his finger movements which caused the deflections. We could imagine what a terror he must have been making the ball do its work at fast-medium pace.

His most devastating bowling at fast-medium set England on the way to winning the Ashes in Australia in 1911–12. On a perfect batting pitch in Melbourne Barnes broke the back of the Australian innings in five overs. He took the wickets of Kelleway, Bardsley, Clem Hill and Armstrong for one run. He and Frank Foster, who was a fast left-hander, accounted for 66 of the 94 wickets which fell to the English bowlers in that series. The next summer in England Barnes played in five of the six matches of the Triangular Tournament. Rain marred the games against Australia, in which Barnes took only five wickets, but in the three against South Africa he took 34 at 8.3 each. At the end of the following season Barnes destroyed South Africa again, this time in their own country, when he took 49 wickets in four Tests. In three series in succession, a total of 14 matches, his victims numbered no fewer than 112. Herbert Strudwick, who kept wicket to him, recorded that on the mat in South Africa, 'He was practically unplayable.' And that enhances the feat of Herbie Taylor in averaging 50 against Barnes in that series. Taylor far outstripped the other batsmen, and even against the modern challenge of Graeme Pollock and Barry Richards he has a strong claim to be dubbed South Africa's best ever batsman.

Barnes' contemporaries united in declaring that he was the greatest bowler, and I cannot imagine that in any other period there has been such unanimity about the leading bowler. Yet he played little first-class cricket; indeed the number of his Tests,

27, in which he took 189 wickets, was not far short of his total for Lancashire and of the number of other matches he played. In all three he averaged fewer than 20 runs per wicket. In Minor County cricket for Staffordshire he was devastating, with 1441 wickets at 8.15, and in League and club games he topped 4000, making a grand total of 6229. Year after year he headed the Minor County averages until he was almost 60. When he began easing himself out of the side, Staffordshire dropped 13 places in the table. In conditions which they knew suited him perfectly Lancashire 2nd XI paid him a remarkable compliment; when the opening pair walked to the wicket, the other nine batsmen were already padded and prepared for an early call to action. That afternoon in the slips gave me every reason to agree with his contemporaries. Barnes was cricket's greatest bowler.

Not long after the war I sat at the same table as Barnes and Alf Gover at a British Sportsmen's Club lunch welcoming the 1953 Australian team. Gover had not previously met the great man. He opened the conversation by supposing that, when Barnes began with the new ball, he held the seam upright and swung it.

'No, I didn't,' Barnes stated emphatically.

'But you used to swing it?' Gover was looking rather out of his depth. However, Barnes agreed that he did, and he was then asked how he swung the ball.

'By spinning it,' he affirmed in a manner to close the subject.

Barnes was not one for wasting words in conversation. In that he resembled Mike Smith, who captained England on tour in South Africa, India and Australia. A depressing custom had grown up which required the two captains in England–Australia Tests to submit to press questioning after each game. It was something much liked by Richie Benaud for putting across his version of events – some cricket writers being inadequately informed. Mike Smith did little to encourage them. I listened to the proceedings once in Melbourne, because the captains came into the press box before I had finished my piece. An Australian spoke for nearly a minute, recalling some period of the day's play and ending with 'Don't you think it would have been better to have done . . . ?' Mike sat patiently throughout. The questioner finally stopped and he replied 'No.' Full stop. The questioner was taken aback but had no come-back. Barnes might have acted in the same way, but such press sessions with captains were not imagined in his time.

Between the wars Sydney Barnes worked for the Lancashire press at Test matches, but the journalist ghosting for him did not get very much out of him. On one occasion at Old Trafford there was an incident which caused some disaffection and controversy. Barnes would not comment on it in print. Similarly Jack Hobbs kept to himself his opinion about fast leg-theory while writing from Australia in 1932–33. Wilfred Rhodes was much the same while being ghosted by J. T. Bolton, a prolific freelance sports writer. On one day of a Test in which India were England's opponents, Bolton was hard pressed to find something to give him a bright story. Late in the day a slow left-hander was brought into the attack, and Rhodes proceeded to criticise and give Bolton the meat to start his piece. Bolton set to work and passed the result to be vetted by Rhodes.

'Oh, no,' he said. 'I don't want to put that in the paper. Just say he showed promise.' The lot of the ghost writer could be very hard.

Off the field Sydney Barnes will be remembered as showing as little signs of the passing years as he did on the cricket field. He was not far short of 90 when I last saw him, and his tall figure was still upright and his back as straight as ever. He will also be remembered for the beauty of his copybook writing, the slope exact, the down strokes thick and the up ones thin, all in perfect symmetry.

On one of his visits to Lord's very late in life Barnes was persuaded by Neville Cardus to discuss current batsmen and how he would tackle them. He was not much concerned with Gary Sobers; he reckoned that his tendency to flick at balls near the off stump suggested an obvious attack to a bowler who could move the ball away from the left-hander's bat. It was another matter when Cardus mentioned Don Bradman. He reckoned he would 'have to work hard against him'. So, of course, did every other bowler, except in the wet, and not many had anything comparable to the craft of Barnes, which emanated from a perfect economical action with the arm as high as it could reach.

Barnes swung the ball either way in the air, and he turned it each way off the pitch. His leg-break was not bowled in the normal manner of slow leg-break and googly bowlers with a cocked wrist, the hand parallel to the ground at the moment of release. In a bowler otherwise bowling with hand upright, that would have made the change all too obvious to the batsmen. Long afterwards Alec Bedser bowled a leg-break similarly. In Barnes' day it was called a leg-break, in that of Bedser a leg-cutter, because the idea had gained currency that genuine spin was imparted only by slow bowlers. My word, as the Aussies say, those subscribing to that belief should have faced Barnes, Macaulay, McDonald and others who could make the ball fizz back from the off. Only the very fast could afford not to use spin on pitches shorn of every trace of greenery.

The cricketing span of Barnes was equalled by that of J. T. Hearne. His first and last appearances in first-class cricket spanned 36 years, which was quite astonishing in a bowler of fast-medium pace. He first played in 1888 and in 1923 he played once for Middlesex against Scotland. He took 4 for 46 and 2 for 18, but the Scots held out to draw the match. The secrets of his longevity were the same as those which enabled Barnes to defy the years, for he had a beautiful method, the easy, perfectly timed run, the smooth delivery, arm again as high as it would go, and no wasted energy at any time.

At Oxford we benefited from Hearne's bowling and coaching in the nets before the start of the season. He had then left 60 well behind, but there was still bounce and rhythm in his fine action, and his accuracy seemed unimpaired. Like other coaches of his period, such as George Dennett, he was always sympathetic and encouraging with his pupils. Hearne was another grand character and a long lasting advertisement for the cricket of his prime. He first played Test cricket when he was 25 in 1892, but such was the competition that he did not play again until 1896. His rivals for England places included Lohmann, Richardson and Lockwood of Surrey, Mold and Briggs of Lancashire, Bobby Peel and Stanley Jackson of Yorkshire. Soon Barnes and Rhodes appeared on the cricket scene, and after 1899, when he was the joint leading wicket-taker with Rhodes against Australia, he did not play again. Twelve Tests does not sound very impressive to modern ears, attuned to hearing about players adding 10 to 12 Tests to their record in a year. As Bill Lockwood played only the same number and Tom Richardson merely two more, the true stature of J. T. Hearne is evident.

Our resident coach at Oxford was Charlie Walters, who was more widely known as the centre half in the Tottenham cup-winning team just after the Great War. That was a Spurs side containing three fine cricketers. Walters as an all-rounder was the mainstay of Oxfordshire, Fanny Walden on the left wing was a long-service cricketer with Northamptonshire, and Arthur Grimsdell, captain and wing-half, was in the Hertfordshire side, keeping wicket and also scoring well. Walters advised and helped unobtrusively but effectively, the right man in the right post.

Another coach I enjoyed at that time was Aubrey Faulkner, South Africa's greatest all-rounder of the period and one to compete with Mike Procter for the title of best ever. He opened the first indoor school in part of the Sellon Works outside Richmond. There he had two nets, and when he shortly moved to Walham Green in West London – the opposite side of Walham Green underground station from Chelsea's football ground – he had four. His big cricket was played before the Great War, when he was among the pack of South African leg-break and googly bowlers. Post-war he made one important appearance. When Armstrong's Australians were carrying all before them in 1921, Archie MacLaren declared that he could pick an amateur team to beat them. The match was staged late in August, and MacLaren's side did win and remarkably, for they recovered from being skittled for 44 in their first innings to get home with 28 runs to spare. Faulkner was the main match-winner, abetted by the batting of Hubert and Gilbert Ashton of the Cambridge side and the bowling of another Cantab, Clem Gibson, and Mike Falcon. The latter was a splendid opening bowler who, like Barnes, played most of his more important cricket in the Minor County Championship, for Norfolk, but was also good enough for Gentlemen v. Players matches at Lord's. Faulkner led the batting recovery against Australia's full Test attack, McDonald, Gregory, Mailey and Armstrong, with a great innings of 155 in only 210 minutes. Against that usually all-conquering attack he hit a six and 20 fours and did not give them a chance. Hubert Ashton made 75 and shared a fifth-wicket stand of 154. Faulkner added six wickets in the two innings to his batting contribution.

He was the best batting coach I ever saw. He spotted a batsman's weaknesses quickly and knew how to try to put them right. I write 'try to' advisedly. The remedy did not always succeed, as in the case of Walter Robins, then in the Cambridge side. Robbie had a very high back-lift, which was an obvious handicap if he needed to get his bat down quickly. Faulkner went to work on that lofty hoist of the bat by stretching a slim plank of wood from side netting to side netting at a height to check the excessive back-lift. Walham Green rang with the sound of Robbie's bat against the plank. Time after time it happened. The habit was so ingrained that Robins could not curtail his pick-up. It remained excessively long throughout his career, which was nevertheless distinguished enough, for in addition to his bowling successes he finished with a Test batting average of 26 and a century against South Africa.

Faulkner was remarkably ambidextrous as a bowler. With the left hand he duplicated his right-hand methods, chinamen – off-breaks by a left-hander – and googlies, which now turned from leg. Bowling and coaching indoors is more tiring than in the open. In 1930 I was on Faulkner's coaching staff and I was more than ready for the end of the day's work after our normal six hours in the nets. Faulkner himself was in great demand

75

and worked twice as hard. Having exhausted his right arm he switched and pitched just as accurately with his left hand. I have seen others bowl with their 'wrong' hand, but invariably they looked somewhat awkward. If, having watched both Faulkner's versions, a stranger had been asked to say which he used in the middle, he would have had to guess.

If Faulkner was the best batting coach, Alf Gover was best at bringing out latent talent among bowlers. I have heard him criticised, for no coach fully satisfies everyone, but I have seen players make remarkably rapid progress under his tuition. One was Alan Moss, who was among the first 150 in 1948 to be taught under the *Evening News* Cricket Coaching Scheme. I saw Alan at the start for, to fit in as many boys as possible, I used to coach during the lunch hour on Saturdays, when the regular coaches were not in the nets. Alan was a round-arm slinger, and it seemed strange that Gover had chosen him from the trials. He had, however, clearly seen something in the boy, and after his first session with me I passed him on to Gover himself, because he had shown himself to be a quick learner. With Gover he progressed so well that six months later he was having a Middlesex trial at Lord's, and he went on to play for England.

7
Duleep to Compton

While at Faulkner's school I bowled to one of the best half-dozen batsmen to emerge between the wars, and one who is little remembered. He was K. S. (Kumar Shri) Duleepsinhji, usually known to his host of English friends as Duleep or Smith. He was undoubtedly to be ranked with Hammond, Leyland, Sutcliffe and the later young prodigies, Hutton and Compton. That he is largely forgotten is due to the fact that tuberculosis cruelly cut short his career.

The illness first interrupted him while he was at Cambridge, immediately after he had started the 1927 season by scoring 101 against Yorkshire and 254 not out against Middlesex. At one time there were fears for his life, but he was pulled round by a Dr Wilkinson at Wentworth. There he practised a cure which enabled the patient to live more or less normally and avoid going into a sanatorium. The treatment was not recognised by the Medical Council. The medicine men had large resources tied up in their sanatoria. By the spring of 1928 Duleep was sufficiently recovered to start net practice in Faulkner's school. He spent three weeks there. At first he was weak and did little more than defend and push the ball around from stereotyped footwork. We felt we were pretty good bowlers, but not for long. By the third week he seemed as lightning-quick on his feet as ever and was thumping the ball in all directions.

When the weather settled he resumed playing for Cambridge,

77

and the next year he played his first Test against South Africa. Then in 1930 he zoomed into cricket's highest realms, England v. Australia, when he hit his dazzling 173 at Lord's. He averaged almost 60 in four matches, and only Sutcliffe exceeded his total of 416. He made more runs than anyone else that summer, 2562, again second to Sutcliffe in the averages, and his total of nine centuries was the most that season. Twice he scored two in the same match, for Gentlemen v. Players at Lord's and for Sussex against Middlesex on the same ground. He played four times at Lord's in 1930, seven innings, five centuries, a total of 679 and an average almost 170.

By now he was a very successful captain of Sussex. They made such progress under him that in 1932 they were running neck and neck with Yorkshire at the head of the Championship. The county season was heading for a great climax. Then TB struck again. Sussex were without Duleep for their last five games, in which they scored few points, and none when they were beaten by Yorkshire in the final match. They finished 53 points behind, 15 then being awarded for a win, although they started that stretch only 19 behind with a match in hand. That was the end of Duleepsinhji's cricket. He had fitted in seven more Tests, in which he scored two centuries against New Zealand. He was only 27 when he played his last match, but already he had scored 50 centuries and made nearly 15,000 runs with an average above 50. He had also hit four successive centuries. Considering the ravages of illness Duleep had the equivalent of only seven home seasons plus one tour of the Australian states and New Zealand. I am confident in my belief that no other England batsman has ever achieved so much in such a short time. Most of the best batsmen have had quite modest averages after seven seasons, taking time to discover the needs of first-class cricket and to get going.

I am also quite happy to go on record with the view that, had he been able to continue, Duleep would have outshone Hammond, indeed every home batsman since Hobbs. He was thoroughly equipped for all conditions and all types of bowling, and he was the terror of slow leg-spinners. Not even Bradman was quicker and more sure in his footwork, and those wretched slow bowlers were hard pressed to avoid being hit on the full toss or half-volley unless they bowled long hops. Tich Freeman was among those who endured the power of his strokes, and in 1930 he had proved his lofty class against Clarrie Grimmett.

Duleep was also second only to Hammond as a slip fielder. He moved like a cat pouncing on the ball. He was not allowed one brilliant catch which would have given Cambridge a win in the 1928 University match. Oxford were hanging on grimly in the last half-hour when Hill-Wood edged a slip catch which was dropping more than a yard in front of Duleep, who dived forward and made the catch one-handed. I was watching from a position in front of the old Tavern. It was a curious illusion at Lord's that the game looked much closer to spectators by the Tavern than to those anywhere else on the ground, wherever the stumps were pitched. All of us there were quite convinced that the catch had been made, convinced also that with Duleep's arm stretched out straight in front of him, a first-bounce catch was impossible, unless the ball had landed far short of him and dropped into his hand lying flat on the ground. Otherwise it must have bounced over the hand. The square-leg umpire should have seen as clearly as the Tavernites, but with Hill-Wood waiting for a decision the umpires ruled against a catch. Duleep was most distressed and angry. As he said, the decision made him seem a cheat by claiming the catch.

I have written much about numerous great and exciting players such as Hobbs, Bradman, Gunn, Woolley, Duleepsinhji, Barnes and Rhodes but, given the chance to recall one of the past masters to entertain me for an hour, I would choose Wally Hammond. He was the supreme athlete, a player of perfect balance and smooth movement, whether batting, bowling or fielding. There never has been a slip fielder since to equal him. There have been many very good ones, including the Australians Neil Harvey and Bob Simpson, but none to equal Hammond's judgment and mobility. His secret lay in his positioning. Against right-handed batsmen he stood very fine, poised to move only to the right. Against a left-hander he stood wide to allow movement in the same direction.

I cannot recall ever seeing Wally miss a catch, and I certainly never saw him on the ground. Slips are often seen falling and diving. Hammond's anticipation and fast moving enabled him to cover more ground on his feet. He took some remarkable catches. Against Hassett's Australian Services team at Sheffield in 1945, from first slip he caught a ball which cleared second slip's right shoulder. Robins told me of another similar one. Robbie was at second slip when a ball flew very fast and low on his right side. Though he dived he did not touch the ball, but as he rallied from the tumble he saw Wally, now on his right side, lobbing the ball to the bowler. 'I cannot imagine how Wally got that side of me from first slip so fast,' Robbie said. 'I never got a touch but Wally made the catch. Fantastic.'

The operative word there is 'made'. Hammond was one of the rare great fielders who not only took catches but made them. Another was Neil Harvey, whom I regard as the finest all-round fielder I ever saw. In his early Test years he excited us by his brilliance in the covers and the deep. Later he revealed equal skill at short fine leg, of which Tony Lock could have been proud, and in the slips, where he was certainly Bob Simpson's equal.

Hammond's medium-paced bowling was marked by the same impression of perfect balance. He took 83 Test wickets and made 101 catches, and his bowling victims included the leading batsmen of every Test-playing country except the West Indies. He did not dismiss George Headley, for he never bowled against him in a Test. Bradman fell to him three times, Ponsford three times, Woodfull twice, McCabe three times and Vic Richardson four times. He revelled against the leading South African batsmen of the period, for he had Herbie Taylor out three times and Bruce Mitchell as many as six. He dismissed India's number one, Merchant, and Stewie Dempster, New Zealand's best. The first time he came against Bradman he bowled down his wicket.

It was the same story with his batting. He was never seen unbalanced, never in an ungainly position. When he was bowled middle stump, he seemed to have shaped so perfectly to the ball that one thought the impossible had happened. Just as he aimed to move exclusively to the right while fielding at first slip, so did he shape to play on the off-side. Early in his career he played a storming innings of 250 not out against Lancashire in 5½ hours. On that occasion he hooked McDonald powerfully around Old Trafford. Subsequently that was a stroke he eliminated from his repertoire. He was so essentially an off-side player that Bill O'Reilly used to attack him with two fielders at short-leg, Jack Fingleton and another. His googly, which got lift from the pitch, was the weapon to use against Hammond. On the off-side Hammond hit with tremendous force. A high proportion of his sixes were hit over mid-off. At Lord's they used to come menacingly towards the top floor of the professionals' dressing rooms at the north end of the pavilion, where the old press box was sited.

Hammond's last great innings against Australia was his 240 at Lord's in 1938, an innings played at 40 an hour. In the course of it he drove a leg-break from Chipperfield a foot or so off the ground. Chipperfield, following through wide, got his left hand to the ball as it winged past but only just. One of his fingers was broken, but the ball was still going so fast when it reached the boundary that it rebounded more than 40 yards from the Mound Stand fence almost to the middle. Hammond was as powerful off the back foot as off the front.

A picture of him driving, which should be shown to every youngster as the perfect model, shows his right knee slightly bent, his body and head over the shot and his left leg from the knee downwards standing vertical. The bat has been carried right through the stroke into the follow-through with arms well in advance of his body. The silk handkerchief which was his trade mark is, as ever, peeping out of his right-hand trouser pocket. He was a magnificent sight on the cricket field. He was a big man with broad shoulders. Everything about his turn-out looked just right, his clothes fitted his frame admirably and his pads looked as though designed specially for him. Even in an age when all players were particular about their appearance he was conspicuously smart. Andy Ducat, Hobbs and Hammond would surely have headed a list of best-dressed cricketers between the wars.

When I first saw Hammond in 1925 he was a tearaway batsman who attacked the bowling from the start. On tour in the West Indies during the following winter he contracted an illness. He spent most of the summer of 1926 in hospital and was entirely out of the game. It was doubtless during that long idle spell that he analysed his batting. If, as in 1925, he could make 1800 runs with an average in the middle thirties, he reckoned that tempering attack with discretion should put him in the 3000 a year class. When he returned to the game in 1927 the discreet blend lifted his total to 2968 and his average to almost 70. He never lost his powers of attack, but from that point he was the finished batsman polished by discretion. He was fully equipped to tackle and tame the Australians in their own country in 1928–29. In the series he hit four centuries, twice topping 200, and his aggregate of 905 gave him an average of 113. Only Bradman with his 974 in 1930 has done better in a Test series.

It was not easy to get to know Hammond. He was not a ready mixer and he could be disconcertingly abrupt. Just after the war he captained the Gentlemen at Lord's, and in his side was a young left-arm spinner from the Oxford side named John Bartlett. The first time Hammond spoke to him was as they took the field, when he told him to take his hands out of his pockets – hardly a tactful way to welcome a nervous youngster. Yet I am sure, from what I learned of Hammond, that he did not mean to be abrupt and unthinking. He could be moody, he could withdraw into himself, and he did not make friends quickly. He probably had little idea about how to go about getting together with a very young stranger under his command.

Walley was a steady whisky drinker, but it seemed to have little or no effect on him. He could unbend, and he could be a

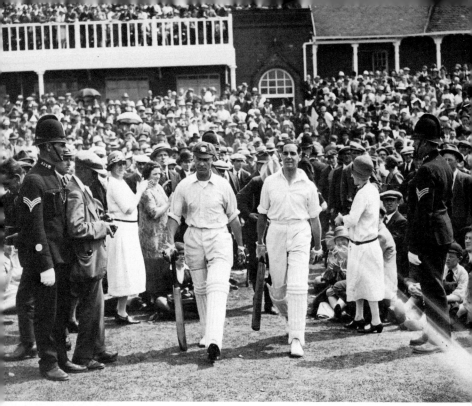

Hobbs and Sutcliffe (above),
their partnership at its peak
in 1926, leave the crowded
pavilion at Headingley – old
pavilion – to share opening
stands of 59 and 156 against
Australia. Thirty-two years
later Hobbs on his seventy-
sixth birthday (left) looks
back on those days of
greatness as illustrated by the
picture of him moving out to
drive – a genuine action
picture.

Maurice Tate (above), who
followed his father Fred into the
England side and finally, also
like him, became a publican, is
helped and instructed by his
daughter, Joan Caruzzi, in his
pub at Rotherfield in Sussex. In
the picture on the right he is the
invisible man. His colleague and
later county skipper,
Duleepsinhji, bats against his
bowling in the nets at Hove
before the 1926 season, when
still not yet 21. That summer he
headed both the Cambridge
University and Sussex batting
averages.

Don Bradman, a golfer of championship class, driving from the first tee at Burnham Beeches in 1948, when he led his Australian touring team in a match against a side collected by Walter Robins. A remaining ambition of the Don was to equal his age on the golf course. 'Sadly the prospect diminishes,' he commented, but early in 1982 he missed by only one shot when going round Royal Adelaide, where par is 73, in 74.

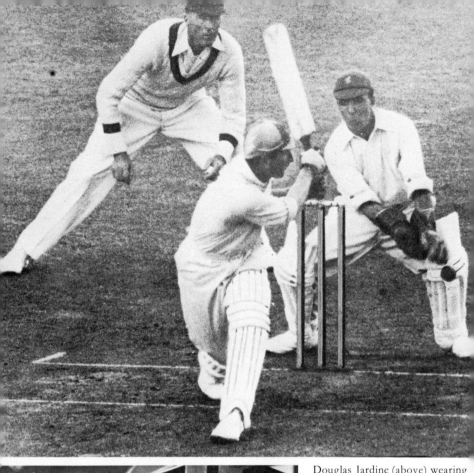

Douglas Jardine (above) wearing the once familiar Oxford Harlequin cap while scoring 74 against Kent at The Oval with Ames at the wicket and Woolley at short slip. A year later (left) Percy Fender, whom he succeeded as captain of Surrey, was seeing him off to India for his first tour as skipper. Fender had been abruptly deprived of the captaincy at The Oval in the tactless manner usual in Surrey between the wars, but their action did nothing to upset the friendship of the two skippers.

Two bowling partnerships. Bill Bowes and Hedley Verity (left), close partners and friends on and off the field, joined the Army together in 1939. Bowes, a lieutenant in AA, was taken prisoner in North Africa; Verity, a captain in the Green Howards, was fatally wounded during the invasion of Sicily. Below, Doug Wright, the kangaroo hopper, is making the final hop to the wicket in the nets at Lord's while Alec Bedser moves back to his mark. In the immediate post-war years they were the only two Test class bowlers available to England, and their toil was hard and long.

Opposite: Lord's in 1929 (above) with coaches used as grandstands for Eton v. Harrow and Oxford v. Cambridge, rather fewer for the latter which was essentially a cricketing occasion. As here the coaches stood in front of the old Tavern and also on the grassy mound behind the low stand bordering the pavilion on the north. Just visible here is the balcony of the Tavern, and beyond are the south clocktower and low stand matching the one above the pavilion. Tavern, clocktower and both stands have long since given way to lofty concrete. Below is The Oval as we often saw it. No, not for a Test but for county matches. This time it was packed for Strudwick's benefit match in 1924 against Middlesex. The low stand at mid-wicket did not survive much longer, nor did the tram (in the background) and its fellows which used to run along the Harleyford Road.

As George Brown and Charles Fry go to open Hampshire's innings at Southampton in 1921 the latter reminds us that batsmen used to trust their skill more than defensive armour against fast bowling. Fry was then 49 and playing his last county season, still wearing the mini-pads – little more than shin-guards – and lightweight gloves of his early playing days in the previous century. With such skeleton protection he resisted the fire of McDonald and made 59 and 37 for the county against the Australians. The grid-iron contrast is provided by the moderns with their crash helmets, voluminous pads, thigh pads, forearm pads etc.

What bowling is all about as revealed by four great fast and fast-medium bowlers. J. T. Hearne (top left) is already sideways on as he is about to launch the right foot into the stride to the bowling crease. McDonald (top right) and Tate (lower left) are embarked on that stride, Tate slightly further ahead. He has reached the position where the power and perfection of his action and the source of his life from the pitch – his body already angled back and becoming more so as the stride continues – are made obvious in this superb action picture. Finally (lower right) the menacing view batsmen had of Barnes, the gun cocked and about to fire explosively. Lucky the young bowlers who had such players as their models.

merry companion. I recall a party at Victor Harbour, a surfing beach 30-odd miles from Adelaide. There were about 15 gathered on the patio of a house overlooking the sea. We were drinking out of newly discovered unbreakable glasses – what happened to them? Empty glasses were being tossed around to test their claim to be indestructible, and Wally was the life and soul of the party. As usual he was with Rupert Howard, the manager of his team in 1946–47. Together they motored round Australia from the time we reached the eastern states until the tour ended, and altogether we were in Australia for almost 24 weeks, twice as long as the modern cricket tourist likes to be away from home. Except between Adelaide and Melbourne, when a railway strike forced the team into the air to pioneer flying for cricket teams, the rest of the side travelled by train. That was hardly conducive to good team spirit, though in fact it was a fairly well-knit side.

The 21-day sea journey between Tilbury and Fremantle, non-stop for the passengers, for nobody was allowed ashore when we called at Port Said, revealed Hammond as absolute master of deck tennis. He caught equally well with either hand, and it seemed impossible to pass him on either flank. Everything that came over the net was returned with interest. Few could give him a game. Bill Bowes, another with a long reach and safe hands, was one, and among the newcomers Godfrey Evans more than compensated for any shortness of reach by his agility. He was here, there and everywhere on the court. The most serious player was Paul Gibb. Wally played only friendlies. He would not enter for the deck competitions, which was as well for he would have swept the board at tennis.

That tour was his last real taste of first-class cricket. He was batting and catching in the slips as well as ever, and he got away to a flying start. Things began to go wrong for him when the Test series started. On the Brisbane sticky his 32 was the innings of a master wet-pitch batsman. Anyone who has seen only an English sticky can have no conception of what an Australian sticky was like before the days of total covering in Tests, with half-volleys rising almost sheer from quick bowlers. It was on that occasion that Bradman was caught by Ikin but not out. From that point Hammond seemed to play the Tests in an exasperated mood. He had repeated cause for that mood, for the umpiring was consistently against his side. When he went to bat in the third Test after Edrich had been given out, his mood was clear. He was very angry, made a couple of dashing strokes and then cracked a low catch back to Bruce Dooland, the leg-spinner.

Happily Hammond's final innings in Test cricket was worthy of the cricketer he was. During the fourth Test in Adelaide he was stricken by fibrositis and played once only afterwards. That was in the first match against New Zealand, when he was England's top scorer with 79.

Nothing perhaps illustrates Hammond's command as a batsman better than his record in the late 'thirties on the Bristol pitch. It had been the victim of one of those, happily infrequent at that time, interferences with pitch preparation by the county committee. They had called in a turf research centre, whose specialists, so-called, introduced sand to the pitch and created a spin-bowler's heaven. Tom Goddard spun the opposition out and Hammond batted as though on a billiards table. In the last pre-war season Goddard took 84 wickets at under eight runs each while Hammond averaged 81 on the Bristol ground.

Hammond also showed his mastery of spin in unusual circumstances. As Gloucestershire left the field once after trouncing the opposition he commented adversely on the batting. Goddard protested that 'it was turning quite spitefully, Skipper'. Whereat Hammond said that he could have played Goddard with the edge of the bat. He was taken up on that boast, and soon he was batting with the edge on the same pitch while Goddard bowled and the rest of the side fielded. The trial lasted for half an hour, and still Hammond was undefeated.

He and Charlie Barnett had worked out the way to play off-spin on a turning pitch from watching Goddard. They played forward only if they could get right to the pitch of the ball and drive it. For defence they relied on back play, and they kept their bodies on the leg-side of the ball. As the ball turned into them they did not play back with the right leg covering the leg stump, but took it outside that stump. There were two reasons. If the ball kicked and caught the inside shoulder of the bat, or indeed any part of the inside edge, it would be deflected into the body rather than into the hands of a short-leg fielder. They further reckoned that, on balance, they would benefit more from giving the ball a chance to miss the leg stump than from relying on the umpire's lbw decision.

Barnett was a cricketer for whom I had particular admiration, not least because I was aware that he disliked Hammond and yet never said a word against him. Indeed, he was one of the greatest fans of Hammond as cricketer and often talked about his great deeds. Barnett himself was another splendidly aggressive bats-man, a genuine number one who set out to tame the bowling and ease the way of succeeding batsmen. He was the opener who set England alight in the Nottingham Test of 1938. Until then it seemed that only rain could check Bradman's Australian side. His spinners, O'Reilly, Fleetwood-Smith and Ward, had gone through the counties, and there was an impressive list of victories, including some by an innings and many, many runs.

Now Barnett brought them down to earth and also inspired Hutton in an opening partnership of 219. By lunch after two hours they had already hit 169, and Barnett completed his dash-ing century off the first ball afterwards. Hutton and Compton each made a hundred in their first Test innings against Australia, and Eddie Paynter, rejected by Allen two years earlier, made the selectors for that tour look silly with 216 not out, the final total being 658 for 8.

In a series which was reduced to four matches by the rain which flooded away the Old Trafford game, Barnett did not last the course, although he had started it so brilliantly. He made more runs than any other Englishman except Hammond on a pitch made for spin bowlers at Headingley. Then he was dropped for The Oval. Another selection difficult to understand.

After retiring from county cricket Charlie Barnett became one of the best professionals the Lancashire League has enjoyed. It was not only his playing success that marked him, for he also took a keen interest in coaching and bringing along the younger members of his club. That was not the attitude of all famous players who joined the leagues. Barnett was the very best type of professional games player, and one who was widely popular both on and off the field.

Following Duleepsinhji and Hammond came Denis Compton and Len Hutton in the 'thirties. I played only golf with Hutton, but I did meet Compton in Sunday benefit games after the war. As one who took liberties with all manner of bowlers he struck me as being a bit fussy, when I used one of his own well-exploited shots and swept a four on the half-volley to the square-leg boundary. The ball pitched about middle stump. Denis threw up his arms and exclaimed at the risky shot.

'What's wrong with that?' I asked. 'It was a reasonable shot against an off-break.'

'It wasn't an off-break; it was a googly.' Compton bowled left-arm off-breaks and googlies.

'Whatever it was, it produced a good result,' I retorted.

Hutton was a batsman in the Hobbs mould, though he was never adventurous and inventive as Hobbs had been in the Golden Age and sometimes afterwards. Hutton also was a masterful batsman on a sticky, and he had all the strokes. Like Hammond, however, he eliminated the hook, though partly for a different reason. A serious injury in an Army gymnasium during the war and a series of operations left him with one arm two inches shorter. He had to adjust, and he apparently decided that the hook had to go. Yet once in Australia in 1946–47 we did see him hooking superbly during an innings of 151 not out against Victoria in Melbourne.

Hutton has often been dubbed dour in his batting. In fact, he usually scored at a brisk enough pace to suit most tastes, and at times he could cut loose, even in a Test. He did so in the second innings of the second Test in Sydney during that tour. In 20 minutes he hit Miller and Freer, playing in place of Lindwall who was suffering from chickenpox, for 37. His straight hitting that day against the fast new-ball bowling could not have been done better by Bradman. Then he fell to the last ball before lunch. He played yet another powerful forcing stroke off the back foot against Miller, but the hand of his weakened arm lost its hold on the bat, which flopped over his left shoulder and broke the wicket.

He treated Miller firmly on that occasion. Four years later, in another sticky-pitch Test at Brisbane, he turned his attention to Lindwall. Though he was recognised as the best batsman in the world on a sticky at that time, a curious decision was taken to hold him back. He batted at no. 6 and was 8 not out in the first innings and 62 not out when batting even later subsequently. On both occasions the innings was in ruins when he arrived at the crease. On the last day Hutton faced the task of lifting England from 30 for 6 to 193. There remained with him Evans, Compton, Freddie Brown and Doug Wright. Very soon he lost the first two, who fell at 46 to successive balls from Jack Iverson, the unusual spin-bowler. Brown stayed while 31 were added, and only Doug Wright remained to partner Hutton. The pitch was still far from reliable, but Doug hung on while Len attacked all the bowlers. He forced Lindwall to place a fielder at extra cover. Hutton promptly drove a four over that man's head, and Lindwall actually finished his spell with a fielder on the extra-cover boundary. Before Wright also fell to Iverson for 2 they added 45, and Len finished with his not out 62 in 90 minutes of superlative batting.

Until Reg Simpson made 156 not out in the final Test Hutton carried single-handed the batting of a side ridiculously over-stocked with immature cricketers. The skipper, Brown, was lying second to Hutton before Simpson's belated success. Hutton's average of 88.83 put him 50 clear of Simpson, and Brown alone among the others exceeded an average of 20. The novices inevitably did little against Lindwall, Miller, Bill Johnston, Iverson and Ian Johnson, and the only other two experienced first-line Test batsmen failed dismally. Washbrook did not want to tour and agreed only under pressure. His play rammed home the lesson that a reluctant tourist is better left behind. He made only 173 in 10 completed Test innings. Even so he contributed more than Compton, who seemed to take his duties as vice-captain somewhat lightly. The Tests brought him only 53 runs with a miserable average of 7.57.

Languishing at home were Bill Edrich, who four years earlier made more Test runs in Australia than any other Englishman, and Jack Robertson, who passed 2000 runs in the previous season and in the following one was to make 2917. Hutton summed up the problem of the side one evening while sitting around a table in the team's hotel. A critic suggested that he should attack the Australian bowling more as Brown used to do. 'There is a difference,' he retorted. 'Freddie Brown is not expected to get runs, but I am. Do you realise,' and he emphasised his words by lightly tapping the table with the side of a hand. 'Do you realise that when Cyril and I go out to bat, we are like a couple of window-cleaners set to work on the top floor of a skyscraper? Only some silly so-and-so has whipped the ladders away.'

He was not far wrong. If Hutton failed, the side was almost certain to fold. He did not deal in failures, but when Iverson dismissed him for nine in the third match in Sydney the whole side fell for 123. In some ways that tour was the peak of Hutton's batting success. To score so consistently well when so much depended on him was quite magnificent, particularly as it was not long since the fast Australian bowling had got him groggy. Lindwall and Miller gave him a heavy dose of bumpers. He wilted under such a fire, as a man with an arm handicap might well do. In the second Test at Lord's in 1948 he was clearly disconcerted, and the selectors left him out of the next match to give him time to collect himself. They were generally attacked, but I thought they took the right course, and subsequently I was pleased to find that Bill Bowes, writing for Yorkshiremen, took the same view. Hutton did compose himself to return at Leeds with scores of 81 and 57.

Inevitably there was much discussion about the respective status of Hutton and Compton. North and south tended to divide on the question. My own view definitely favours Hutton. Given the Yorkshireman's level-headedness and application, Compton might have reversed that judgment. He was, however, mercurial and liked to combine a merry social life with his cricket, and that is not the best recipe for sustained playing success at the highest level.

Compton belonged in the Golden Age. He had the same adventurous spirit as the top batsmen of that time, and he was a great improviser. He would sally down the pitch, discover that his judgment was at fault and recover so quickly that, although still well outside his crease, he would cut the ball he had originally shaped to drive. At times he played strokes which could not be classified, could indeed hardly be believed. In 1947 he was already suffering from the knee trouble which more than once threatened to curtail his playing days. When he played a rip-roaring innings of 246 for Middlesex at The Oval in the Champion County v. The Rest match, he had to retire on that account on the first day. He returned on the Monday to complete his knock. At one stage he moved down the pitch and tripped. As he was falling he contrived a hasty sweep shot and scored four behind square leg. For a man with a gammy knee that was a very remarkable effort at improvisation.

Compton and Edrich, the Middlesex twins, were unstoppable in that season. They headed the season's averages and the Test averages against South Africa. Compton's aggregate of 3816 and his 18 centuries will surely remain records for all time. Greater still was his batting against Bradman's powerful attackers in 1948. He began the series with 184 in the second innings at Trent Bridge. During most of that innings conditions were gloomy and far from ideal for batsmen facing Lindwall and Miller, particularly when the latter dealt excessively in bouncers. In one over he fired five at Hutton's head. Hutton endured the barrage to make 74, but its effect on him was apparent in the following Test at Lord's. Compton, however, batted for nearly seven hours in those difficult circumstances. Finally, shaping to hook another Miller bouncer and then trying to duck it, he slipped on the heavy turf and fell against his wicket. But for that he might just have saved the match.

In another bouncing match at Old Trafford, Compton played an equally great innings. Near its start a bumper from Lindwall struck him on the forehead via the bat's edge. He went off for repairs, which meant a few stitches. He resumed at 119 for 5 and played as though nothing had occurred. His score was 145 not out, and 233 more were scored with the help of Norman Yardley, Evans and Bedser. Alec Bedser was his best partner, making 37 in a stand of 121. His method that day was based on forward play whenever possible with a loosely held bat. The result was that if the ball caught the bat's edge, which it did frequently, it did not carry to the slips. Indeed, Alec scored quite a few via the slips. Those were undoubtedly Compton's most glorious hours during a career which brought considerable glory to him and vast entertainment to us.

Compton was a most casual fellow, who often needed to borrow clothes and bats. In Sydney in 1946–47 there was much hilarity on the famous Hill, in front of which Denis was fielding. The cause was a shirt worn inside out with the name J. T. Ikin on the collar band.

In the early days of the 1946 home season I heard from the no. 2 dressing room at Lord's Compton being refused bats by other Middlesex players. 'No, I'm tired of lending' was the theme, while Denis was explaining that his new bats had not yet arrived. I was still in no. 2 when he walked through on his way to the tea room. I offered him a bat, with which he made about 20.

The next time I went to Lord's Denis was walking towards the Grace Gates. He came across to tell me that the bat was an unlucky one, and I asked him to leave it with Jack O'Shea, the dressing room attendant. Again I was away from Lord's for a time. Next time I anticipated him when we met by saying, 'Yes, I know it's unlucky; just let Jack O'Shea have it.'

'No,' he protested. 'I had another go with it and got a hundred. May I go on with it?'

What became of his new bats that summer I do not know, for the borrowed one long survived in England and in Australia. It finished its days in the museum at Lord's, a fine Warsop bat credited with having scored some 3500 runs for Compton.

Denis was also a successful footballer with Arsenal. He played on the left wing for England in wartime internationals but was never good enough for a full international. He was an opportunist, who might go through most of a game contributing little until he turned up in precisely the right spot at the right moment to slam home a winning goal. His elder and bigger brother, Leslie, was the polished footballer, first at full back and then centre-half for Arsenal and England. He was the strongest kicker of the old heavy leather ball I ever saw. I wonder what he would have done to the modern lighter, far-flying one. Despite being built like a heavyweight Leslie, like George Brown who was similarly constructed, was also a more than adequate wicket-keeper.

In such a mercurial character as Compton, balanced running between wickets was perhaps too much to expect. Never surely has there been another pair so successful with the bat and at the same time so unreliable between wickets as the Middlesex twins. They spent many hours in partnership, but to the very end they were involved in middle-of-the-pitch yes-no-yes-no muddles. With the bat Edrich did not have the same rushes of blood to the head which often led to the remarkably improvised escape shots of his partner, so it is reasonable to assume that the uncertainty derived from Compton, who was a magnet for unusual happenings.

Nothing perhaps was so remarkable as the fantastic dismissal in 1952 at Lord's where Middlesex were tackling Surrey. Compton hooked a rising ball from Loader. He connected perfectly and hit the ball down. It touched down briefly on the toe cap of an Eric Bedser boot at short leg and rebounded to

Arthur McIntyre behind the stumps. Denis was out caught at the wicket via short leg.

It was common practice in some counties before the war for senior pros to father young rookies. Big Jim Smith, the most genial of fast bowlers, was Compton's 'Dad'. Round about ten o'clock Big Jim might say, 'One more half-pint if you like and then bed, Denis.' After the half-pint it was, 'Good night, Dad,' and Denis retired.

Bill Edrich was in Compton's shadow from the late 'forties onwards. He was another who liked to combine a merry social life with his cricket. Accordingly, Edrich's best playing years were likely to be his early ones, while he was making his way and then establishing himself. Pre-war and in the early seasons afterwards, the 'Twins' advanced together with Robertson in close pursuit. Edrich was at his peak in Australia in 1946–47, when he carried the Test batting until Hutton and Compton found their form, and in the 1947 season at home. He scored 3539 runs with 12 centuries while Compton was shattering records, but soon he was slipping behind.

Robertson was one of the most unlucky cricketers I have seen. His batting was as cultured as Jack Hearne's, and he would surely have played many more than his 11 Tests had he been with another county. At Lord's Compton and Edrich took the spotlight. Moreover, it seemed as though critics were looking for something to hold against Robertson, though it was not personal, for Jack was one of the most likeable and popular men in the game. In 1945 he played in the Victory series. He was stationed at Bovingdon without practice facilities. He had to get his practice in the middle against a strong googly attack composed of Pepper and Christofani, right-handers, and Price and Ellis, left-handers. Plum Warner advanced the theory that Jack was not good against leg-spin bowling. He scotched that idea when he mastered Doug Wright playing for Kent at Lord's in 1947. Doug went through the other Middlesex batsmen, taking seven wickets while Jack made 110. The next best was 28 by Edrich. Even at the time, with Robertson averaging 34 in the

Victory matches, Warner's judgement seemed faulty. The next criticism dubbed Jack a second-innings batsman. It was wide of the mark, but even if it had been correct, what of it? First-class cricket is a matter of two innings. His 110 against Wright was in fact a first-innings triumph.

I cannot leave the subject of the Middlesex 'professors' without reference to Jim Sims, a truly great character. He spoke out of the side of his mouth, and often most amusingly. He was a leg-spinner who always looked as if he expected every ball to be successful. When I played against him he was opening the batting for MCC, as he did for Middlesex for a time. He had some difficulty developing his batting on the MCC staff. He and Bill Bowes were close friends and were frequently in the same side for MCC out-matches. On those occasions the two professionals came last with the bat – no. 10 Sims, no. 11 Bowes. Bill was content, having no batting ambitions, but Jim wanted a batting chance. Bowes found the solution: before the next match the skipper asked them their names when they reached the ground, and Jim gave his as J. Morton-Sims. Surely an amateur. He was given the no. 3 batting position.

While batting with Robins on one occasion at Old Trafford Sims was making heavy weather of fast bowling. After one over Robbie asked him 'What's the matter, Jim? Are you afraid of the bowling?'

'Not exactly afraid, Skipper. Let's say a trifle apprehensive,' he confessed.

When he was coaching at Lord's – before he succeeded Patsy Hendren as the Middlesex scorer – Jim listened patiently to a lecture from a brash young player. The burden of his piece was how much the game had progressed since Jim's playing days. At great length he extolled the virtues of what he called scientific cricket, whatever that absurdity was meant to mean. Jim did not interrupt. He waited until the end of the harangue. Then very briefly he demolished the argument that the game was better.

'Yes,' he said, 'you may be right' – a pause – 'but people used to come to watch us play.'

'Scientific' cricket, so called, was killing public interest, and eventually it led to the introduction of one-day overs-limited competitions. They did the necessary financial job, but their brand of play did great damage to playing standards.

Jim Sims died in harness when he went to Canterbury to score for the county in 1974. He was in good company. Andy Ducat died while batting in a wartime match at Lord's in 1942. His last innings was recorded as 29 not out, and when he died, while actually about to face the next ball, the game was abandoned. Eleven years later another Test batsman, Tom Killick, died similarly while playing in a club match.

8

When Blues flourished

A two-year intake of freshmen at Oxford included an English Test bowler, a future South African captain, another South African who had made a Test century against England and an Australian with a Sheffield Shield average of 62. Ian Peebles, who later in the summer of 1930 was to puzzle Bradman, and Alan Melville arrived together. The next year H. G. (Tuppy) Owen-Smith – 129 v. England at Leeds in 1929 when he was 20 – and B. W. (Nippy) Hone were freshers. In the 1931 Cambridge attack were Freddie Brown, who was a Test player that summer, and Ken Farnes, who was shortly to become one. University cricket was very different from what it has since become. Years ago, when the standard slumped so greatly, it should have ceased to be rated first-class.

Ian Peebles stayed only one year, playing through Oxford's very troubled 1930 season, which culminated in defeat by a Cambridge side obviously inferior on paper. Ian took 70 wickets for an unsettled and unhappy side. He had learned the leg-spinner's craft from Aubrey Faulkner. In the indoor school he bowled as briskly as subsequently did Doug Wright, another Faulkner pupil. One day I watched him bowl at a candidate for the Cambridge side in the coming season. The candidate did not know which way the ball was going to turn. Three times in the first six balls Peebles knocked all three stumps and the wooden block on which they were fixed into the back netting.

For a time in the open he found difficulty in controlling his length, but that came when he moderated his pace, and he was only 19 when he first played for England in South Africa in 1927–28. Two years later he left Oxford prematurely to tour there again. Not long afterwards, still in his early twenties, he went in the right shoulder. He could no longer spin his leg-break emphatically and had to rely on the googly at further reduced pace. One of the finest bowling prospects was crippled, though he continued to play for Middlesex with fair results and later took on the captaincy. After the war a German doctor put his shoulder to rights, but as Ian remarked, 'It's come 20 years too late.'

Melville was a polished batsman with all the strokes and a leg-spin bowler, who, but for his concentration on batting, could have become more than useful. He was a highly successful captain of Sussex, and when he returned to South Africa to play 11 Tests he hit four successive centuries against England, the war intervening after the first of them. When the 1929 South African team came to Oxford, Owen-Smith said he was lucky to be in the party, for he thought Melville should have had his place. He could hardly have contributed more importantly than Owen-Smith.

I never told Owen-Smith but at Oxford I treated him patronisingly. He had not got going and was generally batting late in the order. On that occasion he was no. 8 and was caught in the slips off me for a duck. I was bowling when he came in a second time, needing only a handful of runs for victory. I felt that someone almost exactly my own age on his first tour should not risk a pair. I tried to bowl him a full toss on his legs, but it ended wider and decidedly higher than intended, and Owen-Smith swung and missed. I could not repeat that, but I kept the ball wide of the off stump, and soon he scored the winning four wide of the slips. When he was hitting England's best bowling all round Leeds less than two months later, I blushed. Happily only I knew that I had condescendingly tried to help a batsman of Test class to get off the mark.

That match against South Africa was one of the most enjoyable Oxford memories. Herbie Taylor was in the team. He did not score heavily at Oxford, but he batted with every appearance of comfort and mastery. He had headed his country's Test averages against Sydney Barnes before the first world war. He was top again in 1929 with Owen-Smith third. They were as pleasant a bunch of players as I ever played against. One of the most popular was Neville Quinn, the left-arm pace-bowler who died young. There was the happy skipper, Nummy Deane, Cameron, one of the best ever batsmen-stumpers, Bruce Mitchell, their number one batsman of the next decade, Bob Catterall and all.

Catterall was the Adonis of the side. He fielded on the boundary, where he was watched by the girls, and where he could watch them in between times. He was a splendid all-round games player. In one remarkable week at the turn of the seasons one year he was responsible for a treble which could hardly be equalled. He scored two of the three goals by which Natal won the football cup, he ran the 100 yards in 10 seconds, and he began the cricket season by scoring a century. He was a batsman of the highest class. When Arthur Gilligan and Tate shot out South Africa for 30 at Edgbaston in 1924, Catterall came straight back as opening batsman with 120. He made 471 Test runs in that series and averaged 67.

Tuppy Owen-Smith was another of the same ilk. He won three Blues, cricket, rugger and boxing, and given the time he could have added to the list with, among others, soccer. He was a great full-back for England, who made as much use of his brain as his brawn. I can still visualise him preventing what looked like an almost certain Scottish try at Twickenham. Ken Fyfe, a flyer on the left wing, was clean away some 15 yards in from the touchline with only Owen-Smith to pass. He never did, although Tuppy did not lay hands on him. Tuppy would not commit himself to a tackle. Instead he steered him closer and closer to the touchline, and finally a baffled wing-threequarter crossed it.

On the cricket field he was a dangerous leg-break and googly bowler and another batsman, like Compton, who would have been very much at home in the Golden Age. He was not unlike George Gunn, for he too had fancies. In 1931 he played extraordinary cricket for Oxford against the New Zealanders, who had spent the first day amassing runs. A thunderstorm in the night transformed the conditions and Oxford quickly lost three wickets. We were rescued by Pataudi and Owen-Smith, who was not out 48 when more heavy rain washed out the match with the score at 129 for 4. That day Tuppy was in the mood to play all his defensive strokes cross-batted. He seldom offered a straight bat to the ball, and yet he never looked like getting out on that awkward pitch.

Hone, the fourth of the illustrious freshers of 1930 and 1931, came from Adelaide, a very big man with massive hands which were as safe as a cathedral in the deep field. He too was an all-round games player, for he became captain not only of the cricket side but also of the tennis team. In the Australian season before coming to Oxford he averaged 62 as an opening batsman for South Australia, and he hit centuries against the two strongest states, New South Wales and Victoria. In his first English match, apart from the freshmen's game, he faced Macaulay and Verity on a sticky. He had been given scant opportunity to accustom himself to English conditions, and now at the outset he had to tackle the worst of them. He made 38 against that formidable couple while only two others among us struggled to double figures.

That Oxford side of 1931 seems to have contained many men with various sporting interests. Pataudi played three different games for the University, cricket, hockey and billiards. I joined the throng with Blues for cricket and golf, and the curious fact is that those with more than one Blue were all born abroad, Pataudi in India, Owen-Smith in South Africa, Hone in Australia and myself in Egypt.

There have been stronger University sides all round, but I doubt if the batting has ever been excelled. The first six were Dennis Moore, Hone, Pataudi, Melville, Chalk and Owen-Smith. I finished with an average of 26 and was swopping numbers seven and eight with Robert Scott. Jerry Chalk, a freshman with Owen-Smith and Hone, went on to captain Kent, and Scott did the same with Sussex.

That was the year Alan Ratcliffe made the highest ever score in the University match, with 201 for Cambridge, and 24 hours later Pataudi advanced the figure to 238. The contest ended in an eight-wicket win for Oxford well before tea on the third day, although Cambridge spent the first day making 385, which was possible when the over-rate was brisk. It was certainly that, for when the last Cambridge wicket fell two minutes from full time, Oxford had bowled 148.2 overs, an average of almost 25 overs an hour. Cambridge went along similarly. It was a rapid-fire stand of 174 in 95 minutes by Pataudi and Owen-Smith that was crucial. For an hour the latter called the tune. He was going two and three yards down the pitch to hammer the slow bowling of Brown and Arthur Hazlerigg, and he was just as severe on the quicker bowlers led by Farnes. In that time he hit 70. Then it was Pataudi, enjoying nearly all the bowling, who raced ahead, and in the next 35 minutes Tuppy's share was only eight.

I first met Pataudi in a college hockey match during my first term, the Hilary term. A season later we were together in the Oxfordshire side playing the same game. Qualifications were loosely observed in those days and Pataudi, myself and one or two other undergraduates near the University side qualified by being made members of the Hawks, an Oxfordshire club, by J. C. Masterman, the English international and county captain. So far as I know the Hawks, not to be confused with the later Oxford Hawks, played no matches. The club was presumably registered mainly to enable J.C. to recruit county players. For Pataudi a hockey Blue was the first consideration. Much more than a cricket blue it would impress the inhabitants of his state of Pataudi, and he duly won it as an inside forward.

At first I found that Pataudi – Pat or the Noob as he was called – was regarded with some suspicion by other undergraduates. That did not last long. He became very well liked everywhere, and he was the big success of a dinner we had in Brasenose with those 1929 South Africans. The latter lionised him, and he had to sign his name in full, Ifti Khar Ali of Pataudi, on all their menu cards. What ho, racialism! There was none there.

The Noob became largely anglicised in his ways. He absorbed undergraduate humour and adopted our habit of understatement, which did not always go down well with his own people. When he came to England after the war it was as captain of India. Against Surrey at The Oval the last two Indians in the order, Sarwate and Banerjee, shared a record last-wicket stand of 249, and both played quite unlike tail-enders. I was in the dressing room talking to Pataudi when the stand finally ended. 'Well done, you chaps; bit lucky weren't you?' was the Noob's welcome. It was the sort of gentle ribbing he had received often enough in the Oxford side, but it was far from appreciated by his Indian players. They looked as though they could murder him.

Pataudi achieved one of his dearest wishes in Australia under Jardine in 1932. He was the third Indian to play for England, and both the others had scored centuries in their first Tests against Australia. Now Pataudi followed the lead of Ranji and Duleep with 112 in Sydney.

I have often been asked how his son, who captained Oxford and India after the war, compared with his father. The Noob was the more polished batsman and his son the stronger stroke-player. Pataudi senior was somewhat frail, and he was only 41 when he died. After his 238 in 1931 he went out with some Indian friends to dinner and was brought back in a state of collapse – though not from celebrating, for he was a teetotaller and non-smoker. He did not field until after lunch the next day and went quickly when Oxford batted again needing only 55. His health was not good when he captained India in England in 1947 and, although he revealed several glimpses of his best and most cultured batting, he did himself no justice in the three Tests.

Our 1931 side owed much to Dennis Moore, the skipper, who unfortunately developed rheumatic fever and missed his side's triumph at Lord's, where Melville led us. Moore had paved the way and restored the University cricket to firm ground from the quicksands of 1930. He began by organising the pre-season practice, with fielding practice playing a prominent part. He had good material on which to work, for Owen-Smith was an exceptionally quick and brilliant fielder, and Chalk, Melville and Tommy Hart, a Scottish rugger international who was deprived of a Blue at that game twice by injury, were well above average, while Hone was the surest possible catcher on the boundary.

The previous season really had been something approaching a shambles. In advance Oxford had the prospect of Peebles, Melville and Moore being added to ten old Blues. Illness, however, prevented the elected Hon. Sec., Pat Brett, from playing, and his place was filled by Charlie Hill-Wood, a choice arbitrarily made without the correct election procedure by the old Blues. The skipper, Pat Kingsley, was too nice to assert himself, and Hill-Wood with his advisors seemed to play the main part in running the side. By the time Oxford reached Lord's they were in two cliques. One comprised Wykehamists, Etonians and Harrovians, with Neville Ford of Harrow rather unhappily among them out of loyalty. The others were what some of the former group perhaps regarded as riff-raff, Garland-Wells, Pataudi, Bradshaw, Melville, Peebles and Moore.

Dennis Moore was not a welcome member of the side. He had been the outstanding schoolboy cricketer of the previous summer and started for Oxford by making 52 when opening the innings against Kent, but after one more innings in which he made 10 against Yorkshire he was dropped. Moore then phoned Bev Lyon to ask for a place in the Gloucestershire side for their approaching visit to Oxford. Lyon said of course not, because he would be playing against the county. When Moore astonished him by saying he had been dropped, he was welcomed with open arms. Dennis went in first with Dipper, and Gloucestershire massacred an attack from which Peebles was missing. Moore made 206, Hammond 211 not out, the New Zealander Dacre 100 not out, Dipper 81, and the total was 627 for 2. Soon afterwards the Oxford attack endured another hammering and a second defeat by an innings, when the Australians made 406 for 2, of which Ponsford hit 220 not out.

Moore inevitably had to be recalled, but to stay he had to score regularly, and his place in the side was not confirmed until shortly before the University match. The management expected Ian Akers-Douglas, an Etonian with flashing strokes but not enough defensive strength, to fill his place. He could not get near Moore's University average of almost 40.

I was given short shrift by skipper Kingsley and secretary Hill-Wood. In the opening match I took the first Kent wicket but was off after five overs – one wicket for 7 – and did not bowl again. I should have done the same against Yorkshire when I had Sutcliffe dropped at the wicket by Mayhew, who held his place to the end in spite of having a pair of colanders for hands, which spilt chances galore. Again I was taken off quickly and did not return until much later when a couple were thoroughly set. In the second innings I was kept back until Holmes and Sutcliffe were settled firmly in an unbroken stand of 200. A bowler who had taken 45 wickets in the previous University season was surely now worth more than 27 overs. At that I did better than two other old Blues. Bob Skene and Peter Garthwaite each enjoyed one trial only. Late in the season Skene and I were to have played for Surrey against the University, but the Oxford management, doubtless mindful of the Gloucestershire match, refused permission. They had, of course, no right to dictate on team selection matters to Surrey.

The longer the season lasted, the more the side relied on Peebles in the field. The averages tell their own tale – Peebles 18.15, and next Hill-Wood at 33.54. My replacement averaged 43.36! Finally, at Lord's the ultimate condemnation of the policy was the sight of Hill-Wood polishing a new ball and opposite Peebles rubbing it in the dust. Oxford had become a rabble.

In his book, *History of the O.U.C.C.*, Geoffrey Bolton wrote:

Unhappily it was soon apparent that, whatever individuals might do, there was little likelihood of Oxford becoming a real team. Dissident elements were at work and it became painfully clear to the humblest watcher that the side was being run by a faction which, to put it mildly, did not regard cricket qualifications as the most necessary attributes of a Blue. Wellings was dropped after one unsuccessful match; Moore was dropped as rapidly but made himself indispensable. Of the wicket-keepers Inge had one trial and Oldfield none; the preference of Mayhew to either of them was to have disastrous consequences.

In fact I had two games, but with much less bowling than I usually had in one. Unhappily there was not a little of that sort of thing at Oxford in the 'twenties, which accounts in part for our dismal sporting record at the time. Cambridge took the Boat Race year after year, the rugger match and most other games. It was while Oxford's cricket was being brought low that the oarsmen revolted and sacked their President. There was nothing like that in cricket, for either side of 1930 Oxford had two very good captains, Barber and Moore, both from Shrewsbury. Once the latter turned his face against the slightest suggestion of nepotism and put things right, Oxford cricket was kept on the rails by such skippers as Melville and Chalk. Moore was so determined to eliminate favouritism that we nearly missed our best wicket-keeper. Until I urged his claims, Gordon Raikes would not have been tried on tour, for which Peter Oldfield, the probable first choice, was not available at first. Raikes was a fellow Salopian; Moore picked him for the start of the tour just before becoming ill.

Cambridge, of course, were powerful indeed through the 'twenties. Early in the period they had the Ashton brothers and Percy Chapman heading their batting, and all-rounders such as Gubby Allen, Enthoven and Jack Meyer to take wickets. Then came Duleep, Robins, Maurice Turnbull, Maurice Allom and Tom Killick, who played Test cricket while still at the University, and the decade ended with Brown and Farnes in residence. Walter Robins was three years my senior, but I first played

103

against him in a schoolboy match somewhere in Epsom. He was even then top of the Highgate batting and bowling averages. At 14 I was outgunned, but schoolboy cricket was not so easy to find then as now, and we jumped at any chance. That I do not remember how I fared suggests that it was not well. That I took away the memory of Robbie suggests that he did. We were subsequently good friends. Our ideas about cricket and how it should be played and handled were similar, both of us liable to be considered rebels by the Establishment. The Establishment would remain unenterprisingly and dully established without the goading of rebels.

Robins was one of the best captains in the game, a leader of infinite dash combined with resourcefulness. Though Middlesex, lacking in pace-bowling, were without an impressive attack after the war, the leadership and example of Robins helped them to 19 wins in 26 matches and the title in 1947. If his instructions were not carried out, he could read the riot act effectively, as he did when Middlesex played Yorkshire at Lord's. Rain marred the early stages and, when Robins himself and Jack Young had spun Yorkshire out for 187, 2½ hours remained for play on the second day. He told Robertson and Sid Brown that he wanted 150 by the close, whatever the cost in wickets. At the close the total was 90-odd without loss. Robertson and Brown were met by Jack O'Shea, telling them they were to see the skipper who was in a bath. They started to take off their pads, but were told they were to go as they were, to be ticked off by Robins from his bath.

A year earlier Robbie was very angry when he found the pitch for their match against Nottinghamshire was so high on the square that it was almost tucked under the grandstand. He sent for the groundsman, who was a son of Surrey's Bosser Martin, and dressed him down. Martin protested that he had to look after his Test pitch. Robbie half turned, raised a foot to show the spikes and said, 'They will be looking after your Test pitch today.'

One of the long-enduring and very close cricketing friendships was that between Robbie and Don Bradman. He understood the Don. Once we were talking on the 'phone about the draggers among the fast bowlers who gained an unfair advantage over the pure striders. I suggested that there need be no problem if the law stated that the back foot in the delivery stride must be *finally* grounded behind the bowling crease. It would then simply be necessary to state in a footnote that, in the case of draggers, the final grounding place should be regarded as that where the toe ceased to drag and lifted from the turf. Robbie thought it an idea worth pursuing and asked me not to write about it.

'I'll try to get the Don to put it forward, but he won't if it's been discussed, and I shall have to do it in such a way that he thinks the idea is his,' said Robbie the diplomat.

I never heard if Bradman did suggest such a change to Lord's. It was not long afterwards that MCC made the change from judging no-balls on the back foot to the front, a calamitous decision, which has caused the calling of many thousands of no-balls. It is easy enough for a bowler to judge where he is landing the back foot and to keep it behind the bowling crease. It is much more difficult to judge the length of stride and keep the other foot behind the batting crease. It is particularly difficult for fast bowlers whose length of stride varies considerably as they bowl different balls, bouncers, yorkers and so on.

Cricket did not make the best use of Walter Robins after his playing days ended. He should have joined the Allens and Warners in cricket government, but I cannot imagine that such a forthright character was ever very well in with the Establishment. When he was eventually appointed chairman of selectors, he was already sickening for the illness which finally carried him off. His positive ideas were the same, aggressive cricket played to win, but he no longer had the will to impose his ideas on the negative thinkers who were cricket's skippers in the 'sixties. Robbie could not understand nor sympathise with a philosophy based on first making sure of a draw and relying on mistakes by the opposition. All his cricket was played when sides went all out to win and continued to strive for such a result until it was out of possible reach. Then they worked just as hard to save the game. This was the opposite philosophy to that of the 'sixties. Robbie himself was more adventurous than most and a splendidly enterprising cricketer, lofty back-lift and all.

During the 'twenties there were still seasons without Test matches. The main cricketing events at Lord's then were two fixtures, one of which, Gentlemen v. Players, died a natural death when the distinction between amateurs and professionals was abolished, while the other, Oxford v. Cambridge, has shed its glamour. The big social event, Eton v. Harrow, remains more or less as it was, though it is a long time since the old coaches disappeared. Those decorative Victorian survivals used to be parked round the ground, particularly in front of the old Tavern, for both the University cricket and the Eton–Harrow social. I remember one according to its lettering, belonged to a Mr Gold.

When thinking of post-war crowds it seems like another world to reflect on the numbers who used to flock to see the Universities. Though the match was played from Monday to Wednesday, missing the advantage of a Saturday, it regularly drew around 30,000 paying spectators, and the pavilion used to be well packed by members, many of them top-hatted. The crowds are now missing, and a very popular drink also perished in the war. It was a Pimms-like drink called a Hatfield, exclusive to Lord's and The Oval. The recipes were well-guarded secrets. Some claimed superiority for The Oval version, others Lord's. Both were very good and refreshing, and more than refreshing if the first half-pint was followed by a second. Alas, both recipes presumably died with the holders of the secrets. They did not resurface with the peace, like much else that was good.

Numerous potential Test players from the Universities were soon lost to the game. While Chapman and Allen went forward, Hubert Ashton, the brightest prospect of all, was lost to cricket when he went to Burma. His potential was emphasised when he played such an important part in the famous defeat of Armstrong's Australians by MacLaren's amateurs at Eastbourne. His Cambridge career illustrates the spirit of cricket between the wars. It was genuinely a team game, different indeed from more recent years when the importance of the individual has mounted. In 1921 Ashton scored a century against Oxford. When captain the next year he reached 90 and declared to give his bowlers maximum time to win the match, which they did very easily.

Tom Killick, who played for England in 1929 while at Cambridge, went into the Church and was another outstanding University player to be lost. It was the same story at Oxford. Douglas Jardine and Greville Stevens were able to play enough to represent England on numerous occasions. Maurice Allom and Errol Holmes did play in Tests but they were only occasional players for Surrey most of their active life. C. S. (Father) Marriott, who enjoyed one Test, could play only in the school holidays for Kent. Schoolmastering in England deprived Australia of Hone, who must otherwise have become a Test player. Similarly Owen-Smith, studying medicine in London and playing for Middlesex in the vacation, was lost to South African cricket.

9

Wicket-keepers and long stops

At The Oval between the wars a magnificent bunch of professionals deserved more appreciation than they received from the Committee. The loyalty of the latter did not match that of the players. Some, after years of splendid service, were suddenly discarded like soiled clothes; perhaps only Hobbs in that time was able to choose his own time of departure. Sandham, the scorer of 107 centuries, received a month's notice, and by Surrey Committee standards of the time that was generous. Ducat and Bill Hitch, for long favourites at The Oval, were unceremoniously bundled away in the 'twenties and Tom Shepherd in the 'thirties.

Sandham ended his playing career with Surrey not long after Phil Mead finished with Hampshire. He played his last game in 1936, still topping 1000 in the season and averaging 30. While mighty Surrey, one of the Big Six of the time with Yorkshire, Lancashire, Nottinghamshire, Middlesex and Kent, did little for Sandham, Hampshire, a smaller concern, treated Mead most handsomely. They paid his salary until September of the following year and opened a public subscription for him. Mead started at The Oval, was not fully appreciated and moved to qualify for Hampshire by residence. He would appear to have benefited from Surrey's blindness.

There was a story current at the time about Mead's departure from The Oval, but I cannot vouch for its truth. It was said that he was playing in a Club & Ground game and was put on to bowl – in his early days he was a good left-arm spinner. He was wearing his rolled-top sweater and was told to take it off by the skipper – only on the coldest days did bowlers keep sweaters on. He could not because he was not wearing a shirt. Exit Mead from London. It seems a trifle far-fetched, but I suppose anything was then possible with a Surrey Committee. I have always felt bitter about the treatment of professionals in that and other ways, which included Jack Parker playing more than 90 matches before being awarded his cap. Along with that happy Derbyshire team of Guy Jackson that I mentioned, the South Africans of 1929 and the Yorkshire of Sellers, the Surrey men of those days were the best I ever knew in the county game.

One player of the 'thirties did not give the Committee a chance to give him a raw final deal. In 1946 Gover was 38, an advanced age for a fast bowler, even one as fit and strong as Alf. But he came back and played for two more seasons. In 1947 he took 121 wickets and was pressed to continue in 1948. Gover, saying that he was one Surrey professional who did not intend to be cast off unceremoniously, was adamant in his declared intention to retire. Later he and other former players were themselves on the Committee to the benefit of their successors in the professionals' room.

It seems that before the Great War, Tom Hayward set the tone for Surrey's players, and it was fully maintained between the wars. It could hardly have been otherwise with Hobbs, Strudwick, Ducat, Razor Smith and Hitch to set examples. I had a particularly soft spot for Andy Ducat. Not even Hobbs was better turned out, and in every way Ducat was a model for all professionals – and amateurs – to copy. He was, needless to say, a very fine county batsman. He was not quite the class of a Test player in his era, but his admirers were pleased that he was capped in 1921.

Not long before, I had read an article in the *Boy's Own Paper* under the heading 'The Immortals'. They were nine men who had played both cricket and one of the football games for England. C. B. Fry (Sussex), A. E. Stoddart (Middlesex), William Gunn (Notts), A. N. Hornby (Lancs), Sammy Woods (Somerset), the Hon. Alfred Lyttleton (Middlesex), R. E. Foster (Worcs), and Jack Sharp (Lancs) were among them. Now in 1921 Ducat and Wally Hardinge of Kent joined the 'immortals'. Subsequently there were others, Johnny Arnold of Hampshire and Arthur Milton of Gloucestershire, and in rugger Mike Smith of Warwickshire. The honours were neatly scattered among the counties.

Bill Hitch, the cheery chirpy cockney, had dropped out of the side before I had anything to do with Surrey, but I did bowl for Oxford while Ducat was making one of the 52 centuries he hit for the county. Hitch was a bundle of fire and energy, fast bowler, fierce hitter with the bat and superb short leg fielder.

Struddy also dropped out just too soon for me. However, I did see him frequently, and I once went down to Wandsworth for a batting lesson from him in the Sandham & Strudwick Indoor School, which is now Gover's school. Struddy was another of those very kind gentlemen who made playing with and against professionals such a pleasure at that time. He was also the best English wicket-keeper I have seen. There have been more flamboyant keepers since, players whose antics draw attention to them. Strudwick was a very different work-man. He was quite unobtrusive, doing everything quietly and without fuss. Excitement was never going to cause him to make a silly mistake, to which the acrobatic type was prone. Antici-pation and concentration avoided the wild rush, for those qualities carried Struddy into the right position, and his hands seemed to attract the ball. He was essentially a wicket-keeper who stood up to all types of bowler, as opposed to the modern padded and gloved long stop, who stands back to slow-medium hacks.

His hands bore the evidence of his work, for taking the fastest bowling, with gloves in his early years, which by no means gave the protection of the modern gauntlet, left its mark. That fact alone should make all long stops pause and consider the skill of the men who seldom stood back to even the quickest bowler. Struddy carried into retirement hands from which fingers were oddly shaped at odd angles, like a couple of men semaphoring.

Struddy had not long been in the Surrey side when he broke the middle finger of his right hand. He had two rivals pressing hard for his place, and he did not dare to stand down. Instead he rigged a metal plate between the first and third fingers to isolate the middle one. Keeping wicket like that must have brought pain bordering on agony. The protection could not prevent jarring, as all who have batted with a broken finger will appreciate. Struddy kept his place while the break was healing, for neither rival was ever given the chance to oust him. It is usual for broken fingers to be set and given a small splint, which means being idle for at least three weeks and perhaps more. I preferred to allow the finger to knit itself, and then I could resume playing in a fortnight. I was lucky, for though I broke every finger of my right hand, they set straight and a certain thickness of two joints is all I have to show for the breaks.

I doubt if many players have gathered a knowledge of cricket to equal Struddy's, and he made good use of his knowledge to help Surrey and England players. Sandham told me of a remarkable stumping Struddy achieved when he first played against Nottinghamshire. John Gunn, George's elder brother and a stolid performer who was his exact opposite, used to shuffle out of his ground as the bowler delivered the ball. Struddy expected to stump him, but Gunn had always shuffled back before the ball reached him. At last Struddy asked Jack Crawford to bowl three balls straight and on a length and a straight bouncer for the fourth. Gunn shuffled out, had to avoid the bumper before moving back, and by then Struddy had taken the ball high overhead one-handed and brought off the well-schemed stumping. It must have been quite a stretch for him, since he was among the game's smallest men.

Struddy himself told me about his early days before he

became a professional cricketer. He and his brothers worked with their father in something to do with the building trade and joinery. Struddy always had a ball with him, and at every break from work he and his brothers practised catching. Years afterwards, when I used to share with Alf Gover taking our Sunday team from the *Evening News* Cricket Coaching Scheme against London club sides, I remembered that. We could not get the boys for fielding practice. So, every time a wicket fell, I had them in a tightish circle slipping fast and unexpected catches to each other, and it certainly helped to make their reactions quicker.

Hobbs and Strudwick were partners in the running out of many opponents. They were very close friends, and in retirement in the neighbouring county of Sussex they regularly played golf together, still linked in sport.

Strudwick was second only to Bertie Oldfield. He also was an unobtrusive stumper, perfectly balanced and perfectly placed to receive the ball, and again his gloves seemed like magnets. I did bat in front of Oldfield in a game in Sydney which was remarkably advertised as New South Wales and all Australia v. The Press. Well, well, a cut above Test cricket in title! We might have been on the same side, for while I was making 20-odd Oldfield was voicing encouragement.

George Duckworth and Godfrey Evans are the two who most closely challenge Struddy for top place among Englishmen in the past 75 years. George, who was also a small man, was of the same type as Struddy in his work, for he too was quiet and smooth, taking the ball and doing all the keeping jobs well and without fuss. He differed mainly in the volume of his appeals. Until well into the 'thirties appealing to umpires was a gentlemanly proceeding. It was firmly established that only the bowler and stumper should appeal for lbw, being the only two in a position to judge. Rather more latitude was allowed in the matter of catches behind, but if the two best placed to see did appeal nobody else was expected to echo them. And the appeals were quietly made, so that sometimes the first intimation that many round the ground had that one had been made was the departure of a victim.

Duckworth started the louder appealing in England, which in his case developed out of necessity in Australia. There at that time a quiet appeal was taken by most umpires to imply a certain lack of confidence. To impress them that you really thought the right decision was out it was necessary to make a noise. From that has grown the current pandemonium with bowler, wicket-keeper, slips, cover, deep third man and Uncle Tom Cobley bawling their heads off and leaping like demons in hell. Being the sort of cuss I am, that sort of behaviour would prejudice me against the appealers if I stood as umpire.

For several years after Struddy, George was England's first choice. The strength of English wicket-keeping then was such that one of George's understudies was also his understudy in Lancashire. In 1930, when Duckworth was still the number one, Bill Farrimond went on tour with Chapman's side to South Africa, where he played in two and George in three Tests.

I have always held the view that a wicket-keeper should be judged by what he does and not what he fails to do. The best wicket-keeper is apt to have an off day – a human failing. Moreover, there are times when he is keeping beautifully but drops catches. His hands, perfectly in position so that nothing that passes the bat eludes them, may be caught out by a deflection off the bat. Conversely a man may be keeping indifferently but have his hands precisely positioned to deal with snicks. We have to consider also that the most difficult catches behind the stumps are those recognised by spectators round the boundary. If the contact is so thick that the sound of bat and ball meeting is audible far off, that means considerable deflection and a very difficult chance. It is the unheard snick that gives the stumper the less awkward one. If the man behind the stumps continually fluffs his chances day after day, he must then be judged on what he does not do. He gives us little chance to judge him on anything else.

Duckworth was pilloried for one bad innings against Australia at The Oval in 1930. Early in their innings he missed Ponsford twice and Bradman once, and together they accounted for 342 of Australia's 695. After the tour of South Africa that followed Duckworth became second string to Les Ames, who was the number one partly because he was also a first-line batsman. Most bowlers are strongly opposed to a policy which prefers a batsman-stumper to the best wicket-keeper, irrespective of his ability or lack of it with the bat. Both Strudwick and Duckworth were regular no. 11's. However, a good case could be made for Ames. If he was not the best 'keeper in the country, he was, nevertheless, a very good one, unlike some chosen post-war because they could bat, who have cost England dearly in the field. Had he not been chosen as stumper, Ames must have forced his way into the side as a first-line batsman. He was another with more than 100 centuries to his credit, a powerful batsman well armed in all directions. Being the wicket-keeper, Ames was placed well down the batting order, and a man accustomed to the power-house position of no. 4 took a considerable time adjusting to going in with five wickets down. Yet he finished with a Test average above 40.

Of all the wicket-keepers I have played with I would choose Hopper Levett to stand to my bowling. He was another county understudy, to Ames, who kept for England. He did keep in many, many Kent matches, for back trouble often did not allow Ames to keep wicket, though he could bat and field. No stumper inspired me as the Hopper did. The mere sight of his cheerful face above the stumps at the far end was encouraging, and he was one who talked much to his bowlers, urging and encouraging them. He was urging me hard one day at Eastbourne, where I could not get going properly until suddenly the Hopper made a superb leg-side catch and produced a wicket I had done little to deserve. It was said at the time that he snatched, to which I retorted that it was perhaps a pity more wicket-keepers did not snatch. I saw him do many grand things behind the stumps. The one that sticks most clearly in my memory was a leg-side stumping on the old Angel ground at

Tonbridge, which used to be the Kent headquarters. The bowler was Todd, bowling quite speedily and swinging the ball across the batsman's legs to the on side, making it very difficult for the wicket-keeper to follow the ball. The Hopper took it cleanly, and as the batsman momentarily raised his right foot he broke the wicket.

Levett was a great conversationalist at all times. He was apt to be carried away with his own words and neglected to finish all his sentences before starting the next. When driving a car he was liable to turn his head while talking to someone in the back seat. Doing that on one occasion when driving away from a match, he ran off the road, and the car came to rest on top of a mound of sand, a couple of wheels off the ground and spinning. Before the war I used to report the second of the Canterbury Festival matches. I stayed in Folkestone, where the Kent amateurs also regularly went, and the Hopper used to drive me back and forth. If he had any other passengers, I was careful to be in time to sit in front, nervous about Levett's talking habits. It was as well I did on one occasion, when I was just in time with a wrench on the wheel as we headed for an approaching bus. He was quite unconcerned.

Life was never dull when he was around. He was hail-fellow-well-met with everyone and got on Christian name or nickname terms unusually quickly for that more formal era. H. D. G. (Shrimp) Leveson-Gower invited him to play for his team at Eastbourne, and within half an hour of meeting, Hopper slapped his back and addressed him as Shrimp. The old man looked rather surprised but was not unduly put out, for nobody was ever annoyed by Levett. He was called Hopper because he was a hop factor.

Yet there was one time when he aroused the displeasure of the Kent Committee, who were not renowned for a sense of humour at that time. At Canterbury in 1938 the Australians needed only seven in their second innings. They sent in tail-enders, and Levett was the first Kent bowler. When he delivered the first 'ball' to Fleetwood-Smith, a bread roll arrived instead

115

of the ball. Much hilarity all round, except in the Committee room, where it was a Victorian case of 'we are not amused'.

It is sad that the arts of wicket-keeping have been put into cold storage by the modern game. I heard Gubby Allen once discussing whether the 'keeper should stand up or back to fast bowlers. Allen, whose beautiful action gave him emphatic speed, concluded that at most times he did not mind, but if the pitch was sluggish, then he wanted his man standing up. At least, he said, the ball then went into the gloves with a thump to give him an impression of speed and to conceal how relatively lifeless the turf was.

It was Bill Bowes who first popularised standing back for bowlers of pace. He argued that he seldom got a stumping, so there was no urgent need to have the 'keeper close. If he went back, Bowes virtually gained a fielder, for first slip moved wider and almost became second slip. That was a fair argument for a bowler of his pace. Slower bowlers lost much from not having their wicket-keeper breathing down the batsman's neck and inhibiting his moves down the pitch. In one of the later Gentlemen v. Players matches at Lord's, Derek Shackleton was bowling with his usual nagging and run-denying accuracy until Ted Dexter arrived. He stood some three feet in front of the batting crease and disrupted Shack's bowling. Three overs passed before Keith Andrew, second then only to Evans, moved up to the wicket, so settled had 'keepers become in their habit of standing back to all but slow bowlers. In the Glamorgan team Haydn Davies was required to stand back even to slow off-spinner Shepherd. And still they called him a wicket-keeper! A warder exercising remote control.

Godfrey Evans, who soon became England's number one after the war, stood back much more than his predecessors, though he always stood up to Alec Bedser. He was brilliant but not so reliable as Strudwick. He was good near the stumps, superb standing back and the fastest-ever mover everywhere. I never saw another who could react as quickly as Evans.

Two of his more unusual successes stand out in my memory.

The first came during the Trent Bridge Test of 1948, when Barnes chopped a ball from Laker onto Evans' right foot. From there it lobbed into the air behind him. Evans flashed round and launched himself, both in the same swallow's movement, to bring off a highly improbable catch. He was as nimble in forward as in reverse gear. Two years later in Brisbane, Sam Loxton edged a ball from Freddie Brown. Evans did not hold it, and it rebounded towards the bowler, but again with improbable swiftness of reaction and movement he retrieved the mistake. He dived full length down the pitch and got a glove under the ball before it touched down.

After his reign the standard declined sadly and quickly. Soon the game was full of long stops, headed by Alan Knott, who was nearly as agile as Evans when standing alongside the slips but was not good standing up to slow bowling. Bob Taylor was the only wicket-keeper fully worthy of the title by the start of the 'eighties. There was, however, obvious promise in such as Paul Downton of Middlesex, Jack Richards of Surrey and Hampshire's Bobby Parks, son of Jim the second. But whether they would enjoy enough experience in the true wicket-keeping position was the question.

10
Surrey men

Linking the Surrey era of Hobbs and Strudwick with that of Gover and Fishlock was the long-serving skipper, Percy George Fender. He was one of the more meteoric cricketers, the man responsible for the fastest hundred, 35 minutes against Northamptonshire. He was a great hitter, a leg-break and googly bowler who could be as dangerous as anyone, and a splendid slip fielder. It is, however, on his captaincy that his reputation mainly rests. That he was the most astute skipper of the time is unquestionable. Fender knew cricket inside out, and he was a schemer without equal. He made the best use of limited bowling resources, and to augment them he moved fielders around like chessmen. At times he seemed ultra-fussy. During one Gentlemen v. Players match at The Oval Gubby Allen was moved here and there a yard or two at a time. After lunch he took out a piece of chalk, with which he proceeded to mark his positions on the ground.

Not all bowlers could follow his moves and match them with their bowling. Against Lancashire on a heavy pitch, the ball turning but without bite, he put me on and refused me my usual fielder at deep mid-wicket. I protested that the batsman would hit me there with the turn. No, Fender assured me, he wanted him to *try* to hit me there. I did not know how I was supposed to bowl to fit in with his plan. The result was that Ernest Tyldesley hit me there several times, high hits which stopped quickly on the heavy ground and counted two each time. I still preferred the field placings as recommended by Vallance Jupp. They had worked. The Fender variation did not work for me.

That is not meant to imply that I did not learn from Percy George, as most who played with him did. Against Kent our first innings was played on a sticky, and Fender said 'They'll bowl us out for about 100 whatever we do, so we'll get them as quickly as possible.' Before I went in he instructed me about attacking in such conditions. He told me to keep the wrists firm in the actual hitting of the ball, for wristy strokes on a sticky have no future. I collected 10 with his method. We actually made 121 in about 75 minutes, and Percy George was the main contributor with 37. He was not batting for much longer than 15 minutes against Freeman and C. S. (Father) Marriott.

The latter was a Cambridge Blue, who played one highly successful Test in which he took 11 West Indies wickets in 1933. He was a more emphatic spinner than Freeman, and I personally found him the more dangerous. In fact, when it was a case of saving the game on that occasion, I asked Bob Gregory to take Marriott as much as possible. I always felt that I could play Tich safely so long as I exercised care. Yet he got me sooner or later, and generally too soon for my liking, for he was the sort of insidious bowler, innocent in appearance, who induced indiscretions. I knew, for instance, enough about him not to hook his shorter ball, for that was usually his top-spinner slipping through lower than the others. Yet I would hook, and the likely result then was lbw.

That Fender never captained England was a matter of much discussion and controversy. Fleet Street, I remember, often called for his appointment, but in this case the pen was not mighty enough. If Fender could have taken most of the Surrey side into the England team, he would have been the right choice. As that was impossible I think the selectors were right to look beyond him to Arthur Gilligan, Frank Mann, Arthur Carr and Percy Chapman during the time he was at his peak. However, he should on merit have represented England more often.

His overall Test record was modest, a top score of 60 and 29 expensive wickets in 13 games. It would doubtless have been better if he had been given the lengthy run in the side which his skills deserved.

Against Lancashire at The Oval in 1931 Fender came against a professional captain. Peter Eckersley could not play, and Ernest Tyldesley led the side. He came to The Oval determined not to be browbeaten, and the match was more one of debate and argument than of cricket. There was not much play on the Saturday. Before a rain storm Lancashire made 129 for 3 with Tyldesley and Paynter both in the region of 50. The rain changed everything, for when play was again possible Gover started mowing down the Lancastrians. When six wickets were down the batsmen ceased to pat down the marks of balls pitching on the soft turf. The idea was that a fine week-end would harden the surface and leave it rough for the Lancashire bowlers. At the fall of the next wicket Fender summoned all his players to repair the damage by foot, which we repeated at the fall of the next two wickets. George Duckworth protested to Percy George.

'You can't do that, Mr Fender.'

'Show me something in the laws which prevents it,' Percy retorted and continued stamping down the pitch marks.

George then appealed to the umpires and got nowhere. He probably did not expect to, for umpires were usually persuaded that what Mr Fender thought was right.

At the close the total was 153 for 9. It was pouring with rain on Monday morning, when a dispute broke out between the two captains about the cutting of the pitch after a week-end break. The regulation was not too clearly worded at the time. Surrey wanted a cut; Lancashire did not, though in those heavy turf conditions I doubt if either way would have made a ha'porth of difference. The argument was not resolved by lunch-time, after which, the rain still tumbling down, play was abandoned for the day. Precisely the same happened on the Tuesday. Again the combat was indecisive, and again play had to be abandoned to the weather immediately after lunch.

If Fender had been made captain of England, Tyldesley and Duckworth were two of the players he could expect in the side. That is why I do not fancy he would have been a good choice as captain. Those who played for Fender and those who played against him held different views about him. All agreed about his knowledge of the game and his astuteness in using it, but he was abrasive, and the bulk of the England team would have come from the ranks of those accustomed to playing against rather than with him. It would have been very difficult for him to develop true team spirit among players from several counties, mostly joining the team suspicious of, if not antagonistic to, the skipper.

I felt aggrieved when playing for Oxford at The Oval in 1929. I bowled Fender middle stump and we had the mortifying experience of fielding while he then advanced from 18 to 74. All our side, Andy Ducat, his partner, and the next batsman, who came out to the top of the steps prepared to come in, had no doubts. Even the circumstantial evidence seemed conclusive. The middle stump was slanted slightly back and both bails were lying behind the wicket-keeper. The ball had struck the top of that stump.

I went to sit on the grass beside Alan Barber at mid-off. We were chatting when Alan looked up and said 'He hasn't gone.' If I knew what I do now, I would have sat on. As it was I went to the umpire, who said he could not see what happened because I ran in front of him. That was rubbish, for I used to finish well clear of the cut surface; in fact I had difficulty to check from swinging left onto the middle of the pitch when bowling round the wicket. The square-leg umpire similarly 'could not see'. Fender, thinking that Benson, the wicket-keeper, had disturbed the wicket, was fully entitled to wait for an umpire's decision. Our grievance was really against the umpires, Tom Oates, the former Nottinghamshire wicket-keeper, and someone named Sellick of no first-class county.

There is no question that captains have always enjoyed an advantage with umpires, due to the totally unnecessary system whereby the two captains fill in a report on the umpires after every match. Inevitably they are going to give more benefit of any doubt to captains than to others. It was very difficult later to land lbw decisions against Colin Cowdrey and Mike Smith. The system should never have been introduced. The first-class game has few enough teams to make it possible to keep tabs on umpires without regular match reports. Here is a tight little community, and everybody in it soon gets to know the good and bad umpires. Reports were not needed between the wars to indicate Frank Chester as being outstanding, nor post-war to indicate the lofty standing of Sid Buller.

Early in the 'thirties the Surrey Committee ran true to form in bringing Fender's rule to an end. It was crudely and unkindly done, when the Committee thought the time had come for a change of leadership but were apparently reluctant to face Fender. Douglas Jardine, Errol Holmes and Monty Garland-Wells followed him in half a dozen years. Fender was still leading Surrey successfully when sacked. He was still an important all-rounder when he was eased out as a player in 1936. Surrey's results did nothing to recommend the Committee's action after the change of captaincy.

Jardine was another controversial skipper from Surrey. He was the general who directed Larwood and Voce in what Australians termed the bodyline series. The rights and wrongs of his fast leg-theory have long been argued inconclusively. Two Australian batsmen were struck severe blows by balls from Larwood during the Tests. Both actually ducked into balls which would not otherwise have done damage. Oldfield at Adelaide indeed headed a ball which was not going much over the stumps. Those two events do not form solid evidence for condemning the English fast bowling as intimidatory direct attack. There were members of the England side who tended to be against the tactics. Equally there were others who thought that the Australians were overdoing their indignation and squealing without due cause.

It was the presence of leg-side fielders that caused the fast bowling to evoke such a furore. It is clear from the accounts that Larwood and Voce did not bowl an excessive number of bouncers. All agreed that Larwood was wonderfully accurate, pitching on the wicket and slanting into the batsman. On the very hard and fast Australian pitches he was getting lift to hip height, but that he hit the stumps 15 times and had another batsman lbw tended to supply evidence against the Australian case.

English batsmen have had to endure worse from opposing fast bowlers. Gregory was not exactly sparing in his use of bumpers. There were times when Lindwall and Miller fired many more than were justifiable, particularly at Hutton, who for a time was their main target. South Africa's pair of battering rams, Adcock and Heine, kept the scoring quiet by bowling bouncers, and both Australian and West Indies bowlers of the 'seventies were guilty of mounting intimidatory direct attacks on the person. Given the choice, I fancy most batsmen would have preferred to meet the accurate Larwood, bowling to a leg-side field, than a West Indies express battering them from round the wicket.

Douglas Jardine was not an easy man to know. He was quiet and reflective with a very dry sense of humour. I played both with and against him. At first I did not know how to take him. I could finally have liked or disliked him, one or the other, but certainly nothing neutral. After spending a match with him in the Branksome Tower Hotel on the West Cliff at Bournemouth I found I liked him very much indeed. We were alone together in the hotel. Douglas was also very knowledgeable and a deep thinker about cricket, but his style of leadership was very different from Fender's. It was on a much quieter note, but he was just as determined. Both were men of strong character who pursued their aims wholeheartedly and were not deterred by opposition. Jardine had much to disturb a lesser man during that Australian tour. The crowd became inflamed, the Australian players were antagonistic and their officials strongly critical. Jardine sailed resolutely on his determined course.

After one Test innings he was asked who had given him out as he came to the pavilion. Jardine turned and, his arm sweeping round the ground, replied, 'That rabble.'

Among Jardine's most ardent fans and admirers was George Duckworth, who was among the 'camp followers' on that tour, those who did not figure in the Test side. If anyone is going to be against the skipper, it is a player demoted or overlooked for the Tests. That Duckworth was one of his staunchest defenders impresses me greatly. The little Lancastrian was nobody's fool. He was a very shrewd character and a splendid touring companion, as we found post-war, when he went to Australia with the press and later as the team's scorer. Bill Bowes was another who sided with Jardine, and I would take the opinions of those two northerners before those of most people.

Long afterwards, on returning from an Australian tour, I met Jardine in the pavilion at Lord's. He asked me about a certain player who had been very disappointing on the field, and about whom there were off-the-field reports. I filled him in, and he commented on the lack of action by the tour management. 'It's a lot easier than in my time,' he concluded. 'A player can be sent home in two or three days now by air.'

Among the new generation who had the benefit of Fender's guidance in his final years of leadership was one who should have gone to the very top. Laurie Fishlock was a greatly gifted left-handed batsman, but something in his temperamental make-up did not allow him to take the step from county to Test cricket. He twice toured Australia, before and after the war, without batting to his true form, and he played in four Tests without doing himself a scrap of justice. During his second visit to Australia he could manage nothing better than a top score of 57 in 10 first-class matches and an average of 20.56. Cosily restored to the Surrey side, he was a completely different batsman when the Australians went to The Oval the next English season. He played fine cricket against them for scores of 31 and 61, and Jack Fingleton and Bill O'Reilly were sitting open-mouthed in the press box.

'It isn't the same bloke,' they concluded. 'It must be a brother.'

There was as much polish in the batting of the newer players as of their predecessors. Stan Squires, for instance, whose eyesight, requiring thick glasses, was a handicap. Tom Barling was a particularly stylish stroke-maker all round the wicket. There were few better players of slow and medium-paced bowling, but he was not as sure against genuine pace. That was enough to keep him from challenging for a Test place. His opening partner, Bob Gregory, for some seasons must have been considered more than once for England, but the nearest he came was when acting as twelfth man. On tour under Jardine in India in 1933–34 he missed Test selection.

Gregory was not only an admirable batsman but also a fine fielder in the deep and a valuable bowler of a type eliminated by limited-overs cricket. He was very slow and insidiously tempting. He used gentle leg-spin, but his danger came from flight. His bowling was not as innocent as it looked, and those who imagined it was usually paid the penalty. As a change bowler used in moderation he took nearly 500 wickets for Surrey. At one time, when the taking of wickets was more important in general than keeping the scoring down, there were numerous tempters in the game, who made a profit from being apparently transparently guileless. Two or three times I came up against a little man named Sandford, who was then a housemaster at Marlborough. He used to toss the ball in the air, and I fell promptly for the confidence trick. The ball did not pitch where I expected and that was my end. Subsequently I told myself to be patient, watch him closely and ignore his temptations. Yet quite soon I had the fatal rush of blood to the head, and I never did get any score against him.

Jack Parker was a first-rate all-rounder, who was booked for a MCC tour when war broke out. Six years later it was too late for him to have further international ambitions. He was a tall batsman who gave the impression of being particularly upright. His driving was very strong and he invariably scored fast. Yet he was not one to go in when runs were needed fast to gain a win.

Then he was inclined to press for something extra, when his normal brisk pace would have done. He and Fishlock stayed to help Stuart Surridge start Surrey's great run of seven successive Championships.

By then another new intake was in control. The great bowling team of Bedser, Surridge, Laker and Lock, who were shortly joined by Loader, was in full devastating blast. Peter May was heading the batsmen, and again Surrey had an inspiring captain. Surridge had the qualities which distinguished Brian Sellers. The latter had no need to beat the big drum. There were one or two among the Surrey players with a slight tendency towards prima donna actions. Surridge jumped on them quickly and effectively. He even dropped one of his leading players for one match and then got the response he wanted.

I think I should have preferred to play under Stuart Surridge than Percy Fender. One reason is that I have always believed that no bowler should be asked to bowl to a field in which he does not have confidence. The bowler should have the field he wants. The clever captain gets his own way by persuading the bowler that it is really his way. Of all the captains I played under I have the greatest respect for Alan Barber. He inspired complete confidence in his leadership.

11
Cricket from the Press Box

My education, mainly in sport, was completed, and after a year spent schoolmastering, which did not suit me – nor I it – I had a great slice of luck. An advertisement appeared in *The Times* for University men to train as sports journalists. Two were accepted, and by a coincidence we were both from the same Oxford college, Christ Church. The other was David Walker, a very neat and sure fly-half at rugger, who only wanted more weight and strength to reach the University side. We joined the *Daily Mirror*.

Fleet Street, now a precarious work place, was then excellent. The production of newspapers was a team effort in which editorial and printing staffs worked happily together. The printers had their book of rules, but it never seemed to worry anyone. Only printers were supposed to touch the metal slugs and the picture blocks. I did much work on the stone, where the make-up sub-editor indicated to the make-up compositor where to put the various stories and pictures. Nothing was ever said if I picked up things I should have left severely alone. I was doing so only in order to do the job better, and that was our joint aim.

There was a well-developed camaraderie on the stone. When I joined the *Evening News* in 1938 one make-up compositor was a very large, emphatically fat and very good-humoured fellow. He kept a pig in his back garden, the source of much leg-pulling which he enjoyed. There was another compositor who used to break off occasionally to entertain us with a soft-shoe shuffle. He did not do it very well, but he was amusing. There was also a little man named Ted Mead who was on the desk handing out copy to the compositors. Often he rushed short pieces of importance into the page, even if taken to him only five minutes before it was due away. My copy from cricket grounds had to be phoned in 15 minutes before that time. When I finished after the 1973 season, all the copy had to be in the office 35 minutes beforehand. Long before that I was horrified to hear about the antagonisms which had crept into the relationship between editorial and printing staffs, the rule book in the ascendant. Perhaps it was a case of idle hands finding mischief, for all our departments became absurdly overmanned. Our sports staff in 1939 was 17; by 1960 it was 51. And we had less work, with less space available and fewer editions!

The *Mirror* editor, L. D. Brownlee, was himself an Oxford cricket Blue, who played for Gloucestershire, and was also a low-handicap golfer. His father was a close friend of W. G. Grace and collaborator in his autobiography. The paper was a high-class woman's journal with all the best women's advertisements and the famous Pip, Squeak and Wilfred cartoon. Another cartoon character, Jane, appeared about the time David Walker and I joined the paper. She was decorously clothed.

The change came in the middle 'thirties. Bartholomew, a director, was urging the editor to sensationalise the paper. He was a fat little man who wore hats with enormous brims. In Australia they say the larger the hat the smaller the holding. The editor resisted the pressure until he thought he saw a chance to scotch it. A very nasty picture from America of a negro lynching arrived in the office. Brownlee put it on the front page. By the first possible post he received more than 120 letters of protest. He gathered them together and took them to Bartholomew.

Putting them on the desk, he said, 'There you are; that's what happens when I sensationalise the paper.'

Yet within a matter of weeks, Bartholomew managed to get the editor out. A lazy, fat man named Thomas was appointed editor, but he was merely Bartholomew's yes-man who did what he was told. The paper was sensationalised and all the good women's advertising was immediately lost. The first new advert obtained was for Rendell's rubber contraceptives, and Jane took her clothes off – appropriate enough to mark the descent of a very dignified, splendidly prosperous newspaper into the gutter. Within the next couple of years Bartholomew weeded out all of us who were in any way closely connected with Brownlee.

Among the total staff of eight in the *Mirror* sports room, including a sports editor, two men on racing and one on greyhound racing, was an elderly sub-editor named George Winter, who had a voluminous book of cuttings. All manner of newspaper indiscretions and stupidities were featured in it, including a headline reading 'Two Men and a Navvy Killed.' I might have added to the book when I was on the stone with a page almost complete and departure time near. Only a block was missing, but we knew its size. One of the right size was brought and I lifted it to check. 'Here it is,' I said and into the gap it went. A page proof then revealed a picture of a greyhound and the caption proclaimed that it was so-and-so which had been set to carry 9st 10lb in some handicap! Happily, the horse then arrived.

Another floater also concerned racing, a caption gormlessly written for a composite picture which showed a man's head and a horse's head. The caption read 'Lord Derby (left) and his racehorse . . .' There was not much doubt about who was who, and I had the '(left)' erased.

While still with the *Mirror* I had a final fling in first-class cricket in 1933 for Leveson-Gower's team against the two Universities at Eastbourne. Journalism kept me so busy in the previous month, including a job reporting the Ryder Cup match at Southport & Ainsdale, that I managed only one practice session in the nets at The Oval. Yet I enjoyed my most successful week. When I reached the Saffrons, my favourite ground, Leveson-Gower in his usual light-hearted way asked how I was batting. Jokingly I said 'As well as ever,' and I was sent in first! In the week I made 250 runs, including my only first-class century, and took seven wickets.

Shrimp Leveson-Gower had been captain of Oxford, Surrey and England, in South Africa. He was particularly noted as a captain. For many years he organised the teams for the Scarborough Festival, and H. D. G. Leveson-Gower's XI often figured in fixtures elsewhere. He had a humorous face and lived up to it. Once during his Eastbourne matches his team entertained the Mayor, among others, to dinner. The next day the latter complained to Shrimp that some members of his team had peed on the flowers in Devonshire Gardens.

'Sir,' replied Shrimp, 'your flowers should be honoured. Not many flowers are watered with Bollinger 22.'

He was not often stumped, not even while ignorant of the subject when sitting an exam at Oxford. He was then the cricket captain. The first question required him to discuss the character of Pliny. He made a good start, entering his name on the top right-hand corner, putting 1 in the margin and writing 'Pliny was . . .' He certainly was, a long time since, but Shrimp knew nothing more about him. He proceeded to explain on paper. 'I am sorry I cannot tell you anything about Pliny, but I can tell you the University side to play at Lord's.' And he listed his team in the margin.

He was subsequently much amused that even that was incorrect: 'At the last minute I brought in G. O. Smith, and he won the match for us.' Smith, who was more famous on the soccer field, made 132 out of 330 for 6 in the fourth innings. The skipper contributed 41. There were big names in that 1896 University match, for Oxford also had Plum Warner and H. K. Foster, while Cambridge had Gilbert Jessop and W. G. Grace. No, not the great man himself but his son.

Four years earlier at Eastbourne, when in the 1929 Oxford side, I had played against another from the days before the Great War. He was Johnny Douglas, a great all-round games player, who excelled at boxing – winning an Olympic gold medal – cricket and soccer. He led England both before and after that war. I was particularly glad to have met him on the field, for as a boy I had been excited by his bowling at Dean Park. J. W. H. T. Douglas, the most obdurate batsman to oppose Australia, where they interpreted his initials to mean Johnny Won't Hit Today, had been a splendid all-rounder, but at 46 in 1929 he had ceased to bowl – being fast-medium in his prime – and, while his defensive batting powers were still formidable, he had little to offer in attack. I fielded silly mid-off against him, and I was not anxious. It was not a case of won't hit today. It did not seem as if he could. It looked as if he had become muscle-bound. A year later Johnny Douglas was drowned in the Kattegat while returning from Scandinavia. Two ships collided and sank, and Johnny lost his life trying to save his father.

If I could have continued to play after Leveson-Gower's week at Eastbourne in 1933, I am quite sure I could have become established in the county game as an all-rounder. Instead, I was so occupied by journalism that from 1934 I played no cricket until 1938. A gap of that length is far from helpful to a player not yet 25. Later I was to have another break from the game during the war, which wrecked the careers of several professionals. Lancashire's leg-spinner Wilkinson, who came to the front in 1938, played for England and seemed likely to form a spin-bowling team with Doug Wright in the Grimmett–O'Reilly tradition, was one. During the years of war service his bowling deserted him completely. Tom Dean, a young Hampshire leg-spinner, suffered the same fate, left the county game and later migrated to South Africa. In Gloucestershire Colin Scott was a very promising fast-medium bowler in 1939. In 1946 he could not regain his touch but he managed, rather like Tom Goddard, to switch to off-breaks which served him for a time.

In the spring of 1938 I joined the *Evening News* where the

editor was named FitzHugh, a great editor and absolute boss in his own house. He was not universally popular, because he set a very high standard and came down heavily on anyone who fell short of it. Personally I liked him and admired him greatly. I got to know his secretary, a man named Harris, well and I heard much about Fitz from one who was also an admirer. One day during the war Fitz left the office early, deputing one Tidmarsh to act for him. A director named Ward-Price phoned from his office in the *Daily Mail* to say that Tidmarsh should take out a certain story from the front page. Tidmarsh was sorry he could not go against the editor's instructions. He had to say the same when Ward-Price asked for it at least to be shifted from its prominent position. The next morning the editor sent for Tidmarsh.

'I've had Mr Ward-Price on the phone. He tells me you were rude to him.'

'Oh, no,' Tidmarsh protested, 'I wasn't *rude* to him.'

'Then why the hell weren't you rude to him?'

That was the sort of man I liked working under, one who could say what he liked to his staff but would not allow anyone from outside to do so. Good editors at that time were their own bosses. Harris told me of an occasion when the managing director phoned to say he wanted to see the editor. Fitz said 'Tell him I can give him five minutes if he'll be here at five o'clock.' The managing director duly attended, and punctually, on the editor of one of the firm's papers. Among the many reasons for the post-war plight of Fleet Street was the steady erosion of the power of editors, and its transfer to management unversed in the actual production of papers.

From 1934, when I reported my first Test series, my first-class cricket was something seen from the press box. What a decorous place it used to be. There were no typewriters, though they were shortly introduced by Percy Fender, and there was no noisy conversation and laughter. It was a place of serious work, and if any voice was raised rather higher than usual, Sidney Southerton, the then editor of *Wisden*, would look round and say, 'Gentlemen'. However, the press box soon became less formal. It could hardly fail to be more relaxed with such as R. C. Robertson-Glasgow, 'Crusoe' to everyone, and C. B. Fry joining the writers.

There was ample cricketing knowledge in the press box of those days, when papers were produced to meet the wishes of readers rather than, as today, those of journalists. If something was not seen, one's neighbour could be trusted to give an accurate description of the incident. When I retired 40-odd years later, sporting knowledge had come to mean less and less in Fleet Street. In those distant pre-war days I did not come across a single cricket correspondent who was not well versed in the game. Bill Pollock, a club player himself, reported in the *Daily Express* just as Beau Vincent did in *The Times*, though in more popular phraseology.

That does not mean that strange pieces were not written about the game. There was a sports columnist on the *Daily Express*, probably the first of that breed, named Trevor Wignall. Few sports columnists knew much about individual sports. Perhaps they took to dabbling in every sport because they did not know enough about any to concentrate on one or two. Wignall was quite ignorant about cricket. Among his prize efforts was his explanation of the googly: 'So many of my readers have asked what a googly is,' he wrote, almost, if not quite, in those words, 'that I feel they should be told. A googly is a ball which goes one way in the air and the opposite way after it lands.' So now we know.

Wignall was at his most vitriolic on the subject of the MCC, who were then the game's ruling body in England. At length MCC invited him to spend a day with the committee. He watched the play from the committee room at the south end of the pavilion. They dined him and they wined him, he spent the day with them and repaid them.

'We entertained him royally all day, and the next day he attacked MCC worse than ever,' Plum Warner subsequently complained.

'You don't need to start worrying unless he stops writing about cricket,' I urged. Whatever Wignall wrote, and however pungently, a very large number of people read him, and his attacks on MCC plugged cricket among them. The only truly bad publicity is no publicity.

Cricket has been fortunate in its literature. There have been more fine writers about the game in my memory than any other. Golf, my other main love, had brilliant writers in Bernard Darwin and Henry Longhurst. Cricket had twice as many in that class. We have had R. C. Robertson-Glasgow, C. B. Fry, Ian Peebles, Jim Kilburn and Freddie Wilson, father of the Peter Wilson who wrote for the *Daily Mirror*, which he joined a year before I left.

Crusoe heads my list. He was a fine player himself as fast-medium bowler for Oxford and Somerset; he had a brilliant brain; he had a sparkling turn of phrase in his writing. He reported a Somerset innings at Lord's, ending with 'Robertson-Glasgow was then found wanting some yards from home.' The scoresheet showed Crusoe to have been stumped.

When the Test against Australia was played at Old Trafford in 1934, he was allotted a seat with a very restricted view. The old press box at that time had a brick wall on its right side. As the building had been curiously sited to face directly towards where cover would stand in a big match, instead of the centre, a triangular slice was unsighted. Everyone on the front row could see all right. Crusoe was allocated a seat in the third row alongside the wall, which was subsequently replaced by glass, perhaps as a result of his remarks.

His report of the first day's play continued, after an opening paragraph, 'McCabe, they tell me, bowled the second over.' He proceeded to explain his restricted vision, naming the players he could actually see. 'Six competitors – hardly a quorum,' he decided.

There was ample room in the press annexe on the opposite side of the ground in what used to be the Hornby Stand. Crusoe knew that, but the seat he had been given was the one by the wall in the third row of the press box proper, and there he would stay. Not very long afterwards his paper, the *Morning Post*, was absorbed by the *Daily Telegraph*. The latter were excellently served by Howard Marshall, who was also the first radio commentator on cricket and rugger. Perhaps, too, he was the best, for techniques in that line have changed very little since his day, whereas enunciation and diction have become less praiseworthy. After the amalgamation Crusoe wrote mainly for the quality Sunday papers.

The newspaper work of Ian Peebles was also seen on Sundays. It was fine writing indeed, for he had much of Crusoe's facility with words, but for me his finest was in book form. His biographies of Patsy Hendren and Frank Woolley rank particularly high in cricket literature. Perhaps his writing success was some consolation for the early blighting of his own cricket.

Fry is known to cricketers as a great all-round sportsman. He was a cricket and football international and for years holder of the world long jump record. He was also one of the great brains of his time at Oxford, his name linked then with those who became Lord Birkenhead and the Earl of Reading, their surnames being Smith and Simon. His brain and learning were evident in his writing on varied cricket subjects. He wrote a classic book of instruction on batting. In the 'thirties he was writing comments on the main matches for the *Evening Standard*. He greeted a bowling triumph by Bill Voce in Australia in 1936–37 with 'Viva Voce'. And the *Standard* had those two words on their contents bills all over London.

It is human nature to be amused when the great slip. From Percy Chapman I heard of his first sight of Fry at a country house game. Percy was taken along as a spectator and Fry was a player. The pavilion enclosure was surrounded by a very low white fence. Fry appeared carrying a tea tray for the ladies. He hurdled the low white fence, cut it too fine and nose dived, tea tray and all. 'My first sight of the great athlete,' Percy commented.

Freddie Wilson was still writing for *The Times* when I was playing school and University cricket. He came out with some wonderful expressions which were perfectly chosen to paint his picture. He was very kind to me when over-praising a catch I made in the gully during the Schools match against the Army at Lord's. It was almost the only thing of merit I did on that occasion. It is not on that account, however, that I rate him so highly among the cricket writers.

Not many outside Yorkshire are familiar with the writing of J. M. Kilburn of the *Yorkshire Post*. Nobody wrote a better daily account of cricket matches. He knew the game, he was widely read, and he used all he had learned to produce literature. His *History of Yorkshire Cricket* and autobiography, *Thanks to Cricket*, are outstanding.

Most people will wonder why I have not included Neville Cardus in the top group. He was indeed a superb writer, but his cricket judgment was not always sound. It was curious; he knew the game and yet was sometimes sadly in error, as when he misjudged Ticker Mitchell's greatest innings against Lancashire. Moreover, brilliantly as he phrased his accounts, he did tend to mix factual with apocryphal events. An example was his many pieces which amusingly had Emmott Robinson as a character. After Emmott had retired someone remarked that he must know Cardus very well. 'No, I've never met him,' he said.

That I do not include him quite with the Crusoes does not mean that I did not enjoy his work. I did indeed, and for many years we were very good friends. Many were the coffees I had with Neville before start of play at Lord's. He was not only a fine writer on cricket and music, for which he did much, and particularly Australian music, but also an entertaining conversationalist.

Among those to be grouped near Neville have been Jack Fingleton, Howard Marshall, E. W. Swanton and Dudley Carew, second writer for *The Times* before the war. In his slightly pedantic way Denys Rowbotham, my close companion on several tours, was also excellent. He did not branch out from newspaper writing, which was a pity for a wider field would have offered scope for his humour. Few have made me laugh so contentedly. His account of being raped by a husky dame from Brisbane first night out from Tilbury on the way to Australia was hilarity itself. He succeeded Cardus on the then *Manchester Guardian*. Of the present writers John Woodcock of *The Times* may well leave the most lasting impression. He is likely to be the most important editor of *Wisden* since Sydney H. Pardon. One name I must add, that of Bill Bowes. He, like myself, would make no claims to literary merit, but he got to know cricket intimately, and his well-founded views made admirable reading. Another was Arthur Mailey, whose auto-biography *10 for 66 and All That* ranks highly.

Writers of the past had one advantage, for they knew that what they wrote would be well printed in Fleet Street and typo-graphical errors corrected by the Readers before publication. About ten years ago I was sent a copy of a 1934 paper in the Great Newspapers Reprinted Series of Peter Way Ltd. It was the *Daily Mirror* of Saturday 7 July.

The reason for that particular edition being included was the manner in which the story of Fred Perry bringing the Wimbledon championship back to Britain was handled. It began on the front page as the lead story, a staid front page unrecognisable to current readers brought up on very bold headlines several inches deep. Across the full page, four columns, was the banner 'PERRY WORLD TENNIS CHAMPION' not quite half an inch in depth. 'Title Comes Home After 25 Years' followed across 2½ columns, and a third two-line head-ing offered 'MISS ROUND'S CHANCE TODAY'. The entire head-ings stretched barely four inches down the page. I was sent a copy because I wrote in the paper. On page three my account of the first day of the Manchester Test began, 'HENDREN SAVES THE DAY FOR ENGLAND'. The hottest day of the year in Man-chester had us steaming in 86 degrees!

My first sports editor, Barry Horniblow, gave me one valuable piece of advice. He told me to think hard before attacking with criticism. If the decision was to do so, then his advice was to hit hard. To that should be added '. . . and never indulge in destructive criticism without following with a constructive piece'. In other words, when knocking something down suggest something in its place.

There was a stateliness, which may now be viewed as stuffiness, about the quality newspapers of the between-war years. A typical *Times* headline was 'THE THIRD TEST' in two lines, followed by a sub-heading 'An Interesting Day's Play' also in two lines. Now half a century later we see on the sports page of that once sober, but revered, newspaper 'Two Men Who Could Blow Lid Off The Pot'.

Cartoonists have shared the press box with the writers. Between the wars there were several, latterly very few. There have been two great sporting cartoonists. The first was Tom Webster in the *Daily Mail*. He was a master craftsman and a wonderful reporter. At a Test match or football match his cartoon told the main story of the day. He did many great cartoons for the paper. He had rich characters who became his own. There was Arsenal footballer Alex James with his long shorts flapping around his knees, Percy Fender in a sweater stretching almost as far south and wearing large round glasses, racehorse Tishy, drawn with forelegs twining round each other, and billiards player Melbourne Inman with an enormous curved beak. Yet the best cartoon I ever saw was a full length of Douglas Jardine in six lines. From top to toe Webster had Douglas superbly. That sketch used to hang framed in the old members' dressing room, which became an upstairs tea room post-war and then was converted into offices. Webster's Jardine did not reappear after the war, and I could not discover what had happened to it. County clubs should guard their treasures more. That sketch would now be worth much.

The other great cartoonist was Roy Ulyett, first of the *Star* and then the *Daily Express*. His craftsmanship was equal to Webster's, and he had the same ability to hit the nail firmly on the head when picking his subject at sporting events. It would be difficult to separate the pre-war Webster – afterwards he was not the same artist – and the post-war Ulyett. They were both magnificent. I am not sure that Ulyett could not draw heartier laughs from me than Webster.

While with the *Mirror* I covered several sports, even once the newly started all-in wrestling at the Ring, Blackfriars, where I saw the most obviously faked but badly rehearsed farce of a bout. I was the rugger correspondent after David Walker was made Features Editor; I was golf correspondent; I was cricket correspondent. I knew enough about the last two. I played rugger at school and could write about the backs but had to walk gingerly among the men in the scrum. In the intervals I also reported soccer, which I had played as a smaller boy and in which my father had schooled me. A lack of knowledge of soccer did not seem important. Most soccer writers seem to have been short of knowledge. The only one I knew who consistently wrote really well about the game was Geoffrey Green of *The Times*.

Altogether I reported at international level men's cricket, women's cricket, rugger, men's hockey, women's hockey, lawn tennis and soccer. The soccer international was a mid-week affair in which England beat Belgium at White Hart Lane soon after I joined the *News*. The tennis was a Davis Cup challenge round in which Australia easily beat Italy in Sydney while I was on a cricket tour. In addition to the cricket at Eastbourne I did have the chance to play in and report for the *Mirror* two English amateur golf championships, in the second of which I reached the last 32.

Golf was an enjoyable game to report. The professionals were a grand crowd, matching the cricketers. There was George Duncan, an Open champion, who struck so quickly that while blinking you could miss seeing his stroke. He decided on his shot while walking to the ball. Then he took stance, planted the club head behind the ball and promptly went into action. There was craggy Archie Compston, a very big and loquacious man. At a Ryder Cup match two dithering women spectators finally ended their dithers when one said 'Let's go to hear Archie play.' There were the Whitcombe brothers, and I was able to see two of the pre-Great War triumvirate, Jimmy Braid and J. H. Taylor, but unfortunately not Harry Vardon; nor did I see Bobby Jones though I did follow Walter Hagen and Gene Sarazen. And I did report Henry Cotton's greatness when he stopped the American domination of the Open with his win at Sandwich. At the time I was reporting golf I considered the best British strikers of the ball were Joyce Wethered, Henry Cotton, Sam King and amateur Leonard Crawley.

12
Cricketers in khaki

It was no more than coincidence that, as the remaining Golden Age survivors were dropping out of the game, it became more defensive and dull in the 'thirties. That was the subject of an inquiry by a commission chaired by Billy Findlay, former Lancashire stumper and MCC secretary. The Findlay Report of 1938 achieved what no other has since threatened to match. It galvanised the players, and the last two pre-war seasons were so scintillating that they dulled the memory of recent less satisfying summers.

Bradman was in England in 1938, blazing the revival trail. Hammond played one of his most majestic innings – 240 in the Test at Lord's. Hutton and Compton had arrived excitingly on the Test scene, the former hitting his marathon 364 at The Oval. Woolley played his last thrilling innings against Australian bowling at breakneck speed. Yorkshire, making light of lending leading players to England, no fewer than five at The Oval, again romped away with the Championship. And right at the top of the bill was a wonderful Test innings by Stan McCabe at Trent Bridge.

He made 232 out of 300 inside four hours, and his strokeplay was so dazzling that it drew a supreme compliment from Bradman. Most Australians were in their dressing room. The Don called them to the balcony because 'you'll never see anything like it again'. The climax was a last-wicket stand of 77 in

28 minutes with Fleetwood-Smith. McCabe's share was 72, mostly scored off Doug Wright, who had taken four wickets, and Ken Farnes, whom he hooked mercilessly. Jim Kilburn afterwards remarked 'It all happened so fast that Hammond hardly had time to change the bowling.' Bradman was most surely right; none of us present have ever seen anything to match that innings. It was undoubtedly the greatest innings played since the Great War. Whether Gilbert Jessop's hurricane century against Australia at The Oval in 1902 matched it none can say. I doubt it.

McCabe was a curious cricketer. He had periods when he did very little for a batsman of his talents. During the remainder of that series he merely jogged along. His big scores were usually made when Australia were most in need of runs. He began the 1932–33 series by showing the other Australian batsmen how to deal with Larwood and Voce during a four-hour innings of 187. Again his hooking was a feature of fine strokeplay. In that series also he did comparatively little afterwards until making 73 in the final Test.

War put an end to cricket's exciting revival. It had long threatened, but its arrival was nonetheless a shock. It was inevitable long before the last ball was bowled in first-class cricket, and the West Indies team had already cut short their tour and sailed for home. The most unhappy match I can remember was between Kent and Yorkshire at Dover. It was played against the background din of military vehicles rumbling past the ground. Almost continuously a blackboard was carried round the boundary summoning men to report to various barracks and depots. We who were reporting the match were cut off by phone from London after lunch on each day. It was no disappointment that Yorkshire won with a day to spare.

We saw two fine players for the last time. Hedley Verity and Jerry Chalk fell in the war, but each gave us something special to remember. Chalk carried his bat for 115 through the Kent second innings of 215 while Verity was taking 5 for 48 for match figures of 9 for 80. Chalk might well have developed into an

England captain. He had the batting and fielding potential, and as their captain he hoisted Kent well up the Championship table. When war started he joined the Honourable Artillery Company, the same outfit as myself, though we were in different batteries. Soon he transferred to the RAF and won the DFC before being downed in 1943. A year later I lost my younger brother similarly. He won a DFC while bombing the enemy in a Blenheim before and during the Dunkirk evacuation.

I saw one more game in a dull stupor at Lord's while we awaited the inevitable. I cannot remember anything about it, not even who opposed Middlesex, and I have no wish to be re-minded. Then on the Sunday war was declared.

So great was the thing which started, for us, on September 3rd last year, so pervasive of our thoughts, homes, and even of our pastimes and sports, that to look back on the English cricket season of 1939 is like peeping through the wrong end of a telescope at a very small but very happy world. It is a short six months since Constantine gave the England bowlers such a cracking at The Oval, like a strong man suddenly gone mad at a fielding practice, but it might be six years, or sixteen; for we have jumped a dimension or two since then in both time and space.

That was the first paragraph of 'Notes On The 1939 Season' by R. C. Robertson-Glasgow in the 1940 edition of *Wisden*, and a fine example of his writing. He wrote the notes because the then editor had fled London. The position fell to Norman Preston's father, Deafy Preston, who invited his close friend Crusoe to help him. Hubert Preston, deaf as could be and very good-natured, often sat next to him in the press box, where he enjoyed Crusoe's leg-pulling.

Six summers were to pass before the world was again safe for the playing of championship and Test cricket. I am sure not more than a handful of Britons doubted that we should muddle through and eventually win the war. Even in the most depressing days, when the British Empire stood almost alone and scantily equipped against the Nazis and fascists, our confidence remained. Yet, looking back, I confess we had no justification for our belief. In the hateful name of political expedience – the cause of much disturbance in sport also during the 'seventies and 'eighties – our defences were shamefully neglected under Ramsay MacDonald and Stanley Baldwin, despite Churchill's many warnings. When it came to the point, moreover, our faults and mistakes were such that the stoutest heart might have wavered.

In the matter of history I am a sceptic. Most history is written originally to suppress or slant facts in favour of people and regimes. The worst instance is the view widely accepted, on Tudor-inspired and manipulated evidence, that Richard III was a cruel, avaricious man who murdered the Princes in the Tower. In fact, the criminal was Henry VII who usurped the throne without claim to it and proceeded to eliminate all who did have claims. Tudor historians had perforce to fabricate facts to foist his villainy on Richard. It was not possible, however, to eliminate all evidence that Richard was in fact a fine ruler and one too generously forgiving of his enemies for his own good.

Military history is similarly written in large part from reports of competing generals with many axes to grind. We read about brilliant tactics which won battles. After experience from 1939 until invalided out during the winter of 1943–44 with colitis, I am satisfied that battles and wars are generally not won by the victors but lost by the defeated side. We in the Forces experienced British blunders, which echoed those committed between 1914 and 1918. Yet Germany lost again, which does not accord with their reputation for efficiency.

My personal experience of the blundering began early, when 50 to 60 of us were summoned to Armoury House, HQ of the HAC, sent to a gun site and a day later sent home by War Office command. Only at the third summons did we slip through the War Office barrier. We then went to war – the phoney war period – in civilian clothing covered by brown denim overalls.

For many of us military uniforms were months ahead, and we went through the winter in a weird assortment of civilian over-coats, which drew an appreciative crowd for our Sunday parades on Wanstead Flats. What confidence did our motley throng inspire in our amused audience?

The mistakes made and the shortage of equipment certainly did nothing to inspire us. We saw a little thing called an infantry tank demonstrated to a large military gathering on the Flats. It could not negotiate a shallow ditch, but it might just have kept pace with a marching infantryman. There were the many thousands of rounds of ammunition wrecked in gun pits because the War Office initially issued the wrong instructions about changing fuse settings. There was the wastage of time, which could have been better used, in digging slit trenches against air attack in September and October, which were completely flooded when the November rains came.

There was a humorous side to some of the things which went wrong. A very hush-hush square box on wheels arrived on gun sites before the end of 1939. We at length learned that this was RDF, which became GL and finally Radar, under which title it bloomed. In one of its earlier guises it was tried with air co-operation on our site. The square box directed our instruments, predictor and height-finder, to a certain bearing, which it continually confirmed. The guns pointed in the same direction, and field glasses scanned the sky up and down on that bearing. The aircraft remained invisible while its noise increased, until it roared overhead from our rear. The toy on wheels was 180 degrees in error, and faces were red.

Red type rather than red tape was a cause of trouble to us. All secret missives were addressed in red ink in two envelopes, one inside the other. There were masses of secret letters on all manner of subjects, many of them mundane. Yet they also had their humorous side. I received one secret enclosure. A brief letter told me that 'This HQ's S / . . . / . . . / . . . dated . . . need no longer be regarded as secret.' So 'This HQ's S/ etc' was taken out of its secret file and parked in an ordinary one, while the

145

letter releasing it had to be filed in its place among the secret bumph. Which gives us a new definition of secrecy, one imagined in one of those Whitehall corridors.

A typically forthright Yorkshire attitude to the secret files was that of the commander of an independent AA battery, Major Ferrand, in the early phoney war period. One of the occasional sneak raiders set fire to his HQ. From the smoke emerged the battery clerk, heavily laden and proudly saying, 'I've saved the secret files, sir.' His reception was not as expected. 'Don't be a fool,' said Ferrand. 'Throw the damn things back.'

I found the most appealing characters in khaki came from the northern parts of our country. After being commissioned, my first battery commander was Major Fraser-Mackenzie in Dingwall, a man who combined military efficiency with popularity among both officers and men. That was achieved by some territorials but rarely by regulars, who in my experience were surprisingly often neither efficient nor popular. This Scot was an immensely tall man, who alas later proved a target too good for the Germans. His particular foible was a rooted objection to making his men go to church. He often had to call a church parade, but it never got beyond the church – or kirk – door. Shortly before, he had so managed to confuse the timing of the parade at Invergordon that the men had long since been dismissed when the naval chaplain arrived.

My non-church church parade, before I was sent to a troop, was in Dingwall. It was rather surprising that not one man accepted the invitation to fall out on the left and go for a route march instead of church. The men knew more than I did. I accompanied the Major behind the marching column. He asked how many I thought were on parade and agreed that there were nearly 100. As we approached the church he stretched his long legs, while I struggled to keep up with him, and reached it first. There he asked the verger how many could be admitted. When the answer was 100, he said, 'I've about 120 here. Can't pick and choose.' And back we went to battery HQ.

At OCTU in the centre of Wales immediately after the invasion

146

of Holland and Belgium in 1940 we learned that, in the matter of bungling, the first world war antics were the same. Among our instructors was Major Duncan Anderson, one of the leading amateur golfers between the wars, who told us, for example, about his battery of field guns sited in a chalk pit. They were camouflaged with chalk and peppered the enemy for more than two months without retaliation. Then a senior staff officer, one of the spit-and-polish outfit, visited the site, resplendent in elegant uniform, red tabs and all, and ordered Anderson to have his guns polished. Within 24 hours came the Hun retaliation, and 17 gunners were killed. Red tape, red type and now red tabs. Red did indeed stand for all manner of trouble and peril to the Forces.

The red tab blunderers once sent my light AA troop from firing camp at Stiffkey in Norfolk to Perth at the gateway to the Highlands via Cheltenham. We spent a day tacking – and changing trains – across England to discover that we had been sent to the wrong unit. The journey north with even more changes was worse. Two weeks later we were in the Orkneys to discover the ultimate in Heath Robinson military thinking. A key feature of defence against parachutists was two-man pits, manned by a bloke with a rifle and another with a club. Even as late as the summer of 1941 there was a grave shortage of war weapons. When a parachutist approached, the hero with the club was to leap forth and biff him on the head. As P. G. Wodehouse once put it, 'Bean him one, sweetie-pie.' Naturally, the red-tabbed planner in the remote background was not aware that German parachutists wore tin hats and had a nasty habit of firing tommy guns on the way down.

In the Orkneys I was in a bunch detailed to act as umpires during an invasion exercise. We were never told what to do and so were spared contributing to the fiasco to end all fiascos. The Navy carried the troops to the wrong beach on the wrong tide and scattered landing craft on the sands. The Army was not backward in its exercise-wrecking activities. Meanwhile, a single Blenheim, looking superb, for it was a most graceful aircraft, cruised up the battlefield and down it before departing. Below, all was chaos. None witnessing that performance could have been surprised that our first continental invasion trial at Dieppe achieved nothing and squandered many, many lives, mostly Canadian.

Between times I bumped into cricketers to remind me of happier times. The first, apart from those in the HAC, was Bill Bowes when we were fellow cadets at OCTU at Llandrindod Wells. When my brother used to collect me from a satellite airfield not far from the Stiffkey firing camp to take me to his station at Upwood, Bill Edrich was among others on the station completing their training as bomber pilots. My brother between operational spells was an instructor, and he could touch down near Stiffkey while piloting young navigators whom he was instructing. Upwood also housed six WAAF officers, all particularly good-lookers. My brother married one, Bill another.

At Carlisle, Lancashire's Wilkinson, whose leg-break bowling was a war casualty, was a PT instructor, and in Gloucestershire I met Johnny Clay. He was probably second only to Tom Goddard among slow off-spin bowlers between the wars. His type was not much favoured by England selectors in that period. He played one Test only, Goddard and Vallance Jupp eight each. Left-arm and right-arm leg-spin was more in demand. It was generally believed that there was little profit in turning the ball into the good batsmen, that they were, generally speaking, vulnerable only to the ball leaving them. That was a theory which my experience tended to refute. I was quickly put on to bowl off-breaks when a left-hander began an innings, but I had more success against such batsmen when I managed to make the ball move into them. Moreover, Hutton was always more vulnerable to the off- than the leg-break. Several times in Test cricket he was tied down by off-spinners, including the South Africans Athol Rowan and Hugh Tayfield.

At the time I met Clay he had dropped a pip to become ADC to a Corps General as a lieutenant. They came to inspect a battery of the regiment in which I was adjutant. In the first gun pit visited the General took off his almost white raincoat and tossed it to Clay, who held it up and located a smear of paint. 'They always do some painting before an inspection, and the General always rubs some of it off,' was Clay's audible aside.

I met other cricketers soon after I was out of the fray and they were still in uniform or the equivalent. I played on the same side as Nichols, Morris to some of his friends and Stan to others. For Essex he did the all-rounder's double eight times, batting left-handed and bowling right-handed. He was 44 but still able to bowl fast and maintain his pace in that match at Imber Court. Before we took the field Morris told the skipper that he could bowl as long as he wanted, 'But don't take me off and ask me to come back for a second spell, for I can't.' He bowled non-stop from 11.30 until the lunch break two hours later, 21 overs of sustained speed which accounted for the early batsmen. He was a great-hearted cricketer with stamina which more modern players would regard as impossible. Three years after York-shire's opening pair, Holmes and Sutcliffe, had humbled Essex by making 555 for the first wicket, Nichols, with the aid of Hopper Read, avenged his county right royally. The two fast bowlers – some considered the tearaway Read the fastest bowler of the period – shot out the champions for 31, in less than an hour, and 99. Nichols took 11 for 54, the other nine going to Read for 62, and rubbed in his dominance with an innings of 146, 25 more than 11 Yorkshiremen managed in 22 innings.

On the other side of London I played against an army side captained by Tom Pearce and containing Charlie Harris of Nottinghamshire. He was a cricketer who belonged in the tradition of George Gunn, for in his various ways he was no less eccentric. Once, playing against Kent, he took out his dentures, laid them on the pitch and invited Doug Wright to bowl at them. Doug said that he could never afterwards bowl well at Harris because he remembered the incident and was put off by his suppressed laughter. Charlie's contribution to wartime cricket was mainly in a northern league, until he was chosen to play for the Army at Lord's. He declined the invitation and was summoned for interview by his CO, who explained that being chosen to play for the Army was an order, not an invitation, and asked why he did not wish to play.

'I go north each week-end to play League cricket and pick up 15 quid, Sir. Playing at Lord's I get only expenses, and Mr Warner is not too generous with them.'

Harris' explanation did not help him. His Colonel was sympathetic but insisted that he would have to play, adding 'Mr Warner tells me the public want to see you.'

So Charlie went to Lord's and dawdled along at around ten runs an hour during the morning, which did not please Plum. He tackled Harris during the lunch interval but got little change out of him.

'Mr Warner,' Charlie protested, 'You told my CO the public wanted to see me. I'm giving them a jolly good chance to do so.'

Afterwards he biffed a few fours, for he could play several roles as the mood moved him, and got out. The next week-end Sgt Harris was free to go north from the RA Depot at Woolwich to pick up his usual 15 quid in League cricket.

For me cricket had been a rare luxury in the earlier war years, four or five matches while at OCTU, a couple later in Gloucestershire and an invitation to play one in the Orkneys. Happily that was not an official match, and, the ground being perilously rough, I was able to decline. Now at the war's end I actually played more cricket than in any peacetime season since my Oxford days. I came in contact with several more recently arrived players. One I met with particular pleasure was Harold Gimblett, who in 1935 hit a century against Essex in 63 minutes in the first innings of his first match for Somerset. That remarkable knock won him the Lawrence Trophy for the season's fastest hundred. Now at Lord's, after Laurie Fishlock had scored a century for the Buccaneers, Harold did the same for the West of England. As a bowler I had a close view of him. He was, of course, a most attractive batsman, but it was as a splendid companion with whom to play cricket that I remember him particularly.

He did play Test cricket, but the war came at the worst time for him and he never enjoyed a Test tour. That was unfortunate, for he would have been an asset to any side. The six war years were fatal. He was chosen once afterwards to play for England, but he arrived on the eve of the match with a vast carbuncle on the back of his neck and was automatically ruled out. Even then, suffering as he was, Harold remained his usual cheerful self. He deserved other Test chances at that time, for while the 1946 team was being chosen he scored nearly 2000 runs and averaged almost 50. Somerset was a long way away and her players were apt to escape proper notice. They were not alone in suffering that fate. Of all our opening bowlers in the first 20 post-war years Les Jackson of Derbyshire was the most feared and respected by opposing opening batsmen. Yet he played only twice for England. Selectors, critics and all overlooked his claims, for which we really can put forward no excuse.

End-of-war cricket also gave me a match against the Australian Imperial Forces, captained by Lindsay Hassett, at the Saffrons in Eastbourne. That was my luckiest ground, and it was so that day, when the pitch lacked its benign peacetime character. It was a very low-scoring match, which the Australians won by a single wicket against our total of 128. Luck was certainly on my side that day, for I have clear recollection of playing and missing close outside the off-stump, particularly against Ces Pepper's leg-breaks and googlies. He cussed and cussed at his bad luck. Then at the lunch table he came and sat beside me, and his cricket complaints were cheerfully forgotten – until the afternoon session. The luck held, for Pepper in favourable circumstances gathered one wicket only, while my 47 was the highest score in the match. Curiously, I also enjoyed a good day while Gimblett was making his hundred at Lord's, for, after being dismissed for a duck at no. 3, that was one of the few post-war occasions when my bowling functioned well and I took 5 for 58. I recall that bowling particularly, for my first success was against

Tom Barling, with whom I had played in the Surrey side. He was caught at second slip in my second over from an off-spinner which swung much to the off. With the new ball it was always good policy to spin a couple each over from the start. If the hand was turned sideways instead of being behind the ball, the result was often later and more appreciable away-swing than was achieved by other means. Sydney Barnes, of course, never used any other means to achieve swing.

While at OCTU Desmond Eagar was an opponent. He was skipper of the South Wales Borderers whom we visited. Desmond followed me into the Cheltenham College and Oxford sides, ten years or so behind me. Now the pair from the same stable were in opposition, and the scoresheets read:

Capt. E. D. R. Eagar b Wellings   0.
Cadet E. M. Wellings lbw b Eagar   0.

We remained good friends.

In one sense Desmond's cricket was a war casualty. In the Gloucestershire side he had been a spirited batsman with fine strokes and the urge to use them freely, to our considerable entertainment. At the war's end he joined Hampshire as captain-secretary. At the time the county were short of solid batting, and Eagar changed his methods to act as stuffing. His motives were excellent, but I always thought he was wrong to sacrifice his natural bent for attack. His bat served Hampshire well enough, but in his aggressive style he might have done even more. As secretary of a struggling county he was outstanding. Surely no county has had a secretary so devoted as Eagar was to his adopted Hampshire. By visiting all parts of the county night after night he increased the membership remarkably year after year. He worked like that for a salary few others would have accepted, for he knew Hampshire's shortages were not limited to solid batting.

Shortly before my time in the Army ended occurred the most bizarre event to underline the strange way in which Whitehall tackled war. One of our light AA detachments shot down a hedge-hopping plane over open sights with the Bofors gun, a fine achievement by the sergeant in command. Soon, however, 11 senior officers, oozing gold braid and red tabs, descended on the site to inquire why the Kerrison predictor had not been used. Some high-up – high-ups, perhaps – had an interest in that lovely firing-camp toy, which on active service was a useless liability, for the Germans flew either far above the modest range of the Bofors or very low at top speed. In that event they were not in sight long enough to allow the Kerrison to be brought into use. Only the top brass seemed ignorant of that fact.

I also saw blundering by the Navy and RAF. The Navy botched arrangements for POW's I was to escort from Scapa Flow to Inverness. Confusion began with us finding that the Naval Intelligence Officer had not been told about the prisoners, which caused considerable delay. It proceeded with HMS *Shropshire* issuing a list of the prisoners on paper with the ship's name at the top, after insisting that the one fact which must at all costs be concealed was the ship from which we had collected them. If that news reached Germany their codes, which we knew, would have been changed for the area in which the *Shropshire* had been operating.

Security in the RAF could similarly err. One evening, while spending a week-end with my brother at Upwood, four of us visited a nearby fighter station at Wyton. We were driven by a Flight-Lieutenant Sowerby. At the entrance to Wyton he leaned out of the window and called 'Sowerby'. The corporal on guard stepped back and saluted. We proceeded inside, and I remarked to Sowerby that he seemed to be very well known there.

'No,' he said. 'I've never been here before.'

Would someone leaning out of a car window and calling 'Goering' with sufficient conviction and authority have been admitted?

Yet, scrambling through, we did win that war.

13
Starting again

Devoted elderly enthusiasts kept cricket staggering along locally through the war years. Through most of the darkest days Plum Warner organised it at Lord's as a morale-booster. One match was cancelled in 1940 when Holland and Belgium were invaded. I know because two of us travelled from Aberporth firing camp to play for the HAC. We had a full side with first-class experience, and the City of London Yeomanry, our would-be opponents, were spear-headed by Gubby Allen and Errol Holmes.

By 1944 the tensions had eased. We had the sniff of victory and could enjoy week-end cricket without feeling guilty. We were stung that summer by flying bombs, which droned across the sky and became silent when about to fall. Two came near Lord's during matches, the first landing in the north-west corner of Regent's Park. The players dropped to the ground, and Jack Robertson re-started the game by hitting the next ball from Bob Wyatt for six.

It was easy to sympathise with professionals who struggled afterwards to regain their true form. I was fit to play in 1944, when batting returned to me more quickly than bowling. The latter never did pick up all the threads, though it had its days. One of those I now played with at Lord's was Doug Wright, with whom I shared the wickets, though unequally with three to his six. He picked up his threads, though I suspect the long period of cricket starvation prevented him from becoming a very great bowler. He was unusually swift for his type and was surely the only googly bowler able to bowl a bouncer. He did not use it in the middle, but I saw him fire two or three in the nets at Lord's, and they were really good ones. Doug spun the ball hard, which not all English leg-spinners did, from a bounding run, which used to be compared with a kangaroo's hopping.

Match-winning qualities when judged by the rate of dismissals put Wright out in front. In 1939, when we were experimenting with the eight-ball over, he averaged just under 31 balls per wicket for Kent. Of Yorkshire's two match-winners Verity averaged eight and Bowes 14 balls more, which still left them with a fine average. In his best post-war season Doug was still dismissing county batsmen at a rate below six overs, which at the then brisk over-rate meant roughly seven wickets at his end in four hours.

Opinions about Wright's standing varied greatly, for his 108 Test wickets were more costly than his admirers would expect. I rated him very highly. He beat the bat and the stumps, plus the wicket-keeper at times, more often than anyone. In that respect he was unlucky, as he was in the matter of dropped catches, like his earlier namesake in the Kent side, opening bowler Charlie Wright. If Kent dropped a catch it was about evens that the bowler was Charlie, but his cheerfulness was never diminished.

Two missed catches denied Doug something near to cricket immortality. In the painfully exciting Leeds Test of 1938 he had the Australians on the run. They needed only 107, but he removed Bradman and McCabe in quick succession, and four were out for 61. Hassett, the next batsman, promptly edged him to gully. Alas, Verity wrongly anticipated the stroke by moving to his right. The catch went the other way, and Verity's outstretched left hand could not grasp it. Hassett made 33 to ensure Australia's win. Wright took 3 for 26, but what might his figures have been?

Nine years later in Sydney he again had fame snatched from him. He bowled out Australia with 7 for 105 and threatened to do so again. Fibrositis kept Hammond out of the match, and Edrich, normally very safe, was at first slip. Bradman had made only two when he edged Doug straight to Edrich. The ball dropped, Bradman went forward to 63, and Australia scored the necessary 214 for five wickets.

Wright's Test figures should be judged with the formidable strength of Australian batting in mind. Before the war their first six were Fingleton, Brown, Bradman, McCabe, Hassett and Badcock or Barnes, afterwards Barnes, Morris, Bradman, Hassett, Miller and McCool, while Neil Harvey soon increased their strength. At the same time South Africa had a wealth of batting. Wright's playing period was not ideal, for he had tough Test opposition and the loss of six vital years when he was coming to his peak.

Umpires no less than players included their quota of characters, among them Bill Reeves of Essex, who had liked to bowl at 'the fancy caps', the amateurs. He riled McDonald once by refusing three lbw appeals. McDonald asked the reason for the third, and Bill said the ball was going too high. Two or three balls later one again struck the batsman's pad, and Reeves anticipated the appeal. 'Not out, too low,' he called.

He was standing during a game which was not going well for Middlesex. Robins put himself on and chucked his sweater to Reeves, who caught it and asked what he should do with it.

'Stuff it up.'

'What, swords and all?' asked Reeves, holding up the sweater and looking at its scimitars of dark blue stitching.

Alec Skelding, former fast-medium bowler from Leicestershire, was another grand character. He wore very thick pebble glasses, and it was suspected that he did not see too well even with them, but it was also agreed that there was little wrong with his decisions. His weakness was arithmetic. Once he allowed 11 balls in the over. The sixth took a wicket, and when the new batsman arrived he resumed counting at two.

In those early post-war years I met some of the newer players in a series of Sunday benefit matches at Stanmore. The first was for Frank Chester's benefit in 1947. Against us were several from Middlesex, headed by Compton and Edrich, and the Bedser twins and Laker came from Surrey. My luck was in, for I made 50-odd, and a fast bowler formerly in the Lancashire League bowled us to a shock two-run win. In subsequent years against much the same opposition we paid for our temerity. I was more interested in the off-spin bowling than in Alec Bedser. Laker had not yet fully developed his craft and his flight was still rather plain, so that I found Eric Bedser's rounded flight more testing.

A year later we started the *Evening News* Cricket Coaching Scheme, which produced some 15 county professionals, headed by Alan Moss, Brian Taylor and Alan Dixon. While that was running I had further evidence that the top players are often unaware of how they actually play. We had film shots taken of our youngsters, and I used some stills for an instructional series. It began with the grip and pick-up. I wrote that in the latter the right elbow should remain close to the body. Bill Edrich 'phoned to tell me about a 'bad mistake'. He said the right elbow should be well away from the body. The next day I stood behind the net at Lord's while he practised. His right elbow stayed close, and after a few balls he turned to me. 'I'm astonished,' he said. 'I could have sworn my elbow went well away from my body when I picked up the bat.' I suggested he should try it and see how he managed then with the right wrist locked.

My horizon was greatly widened after the war. A new experience was reporting a Women's Test in Melbourne in 1969. Without seeing that match I would not have believed that women, lacking men's physical advantages, could play such high-class cricket. There were three English girls who threw further than I could. However, I did think their game could be even better with a pitch of 21 instead of 22 yards. England were led by Rachael Heyhoe, a splendid buccaneering batsman given to improvising in the Compton manner. Australia had a left-arm medium-paced bowler, Mrs Jean Gordon, who had a most beautiful rhythmic action.

157

Good actions in the 'sixties were already becoming scarcer, although Fred Trueman was still there to show them how to do it. About that time Richie Benaud played a Sunday Charity match in which Bill Voce, then in the advanced veteran stage, bowled. Benaud was full of talk in the press box next day about the beauty of Voce's action. 'I suppose it caused much stir at the time,' he said.

I had to say, 'Not particularly,' for he was only one of many. The actions of some, McDonald, Tate, Larwood and Allen, I thought, were even better, and there were very few open-chesters. Fred Root, Worcestershire's leg-theory bowler, was one, and in our first post-war touring team Dick Pollard was slightly open. Neither established himself at the top.

Australian bowlers at the time of Lindwall, Miller and Bill Johnston, whose method was not unlike that of Voce, had excellent actions. Yet they were succeeded among pace-bowlers by a breed of open-chested chuckers in the late 'fifties. Meckiff was the most widely known thrower, but every state had them, except Queensland, where Lindwall's example kept them on the sideways straight and narrow. Slater in Western Australia, Hitchcock and Tretheway – known to our side as Pitchcock and Trethrowy – in South Australia, Meckiff in Victoria and Rorke in NSW were the most prominent.

England's first great bowler post-war was Alec Bedser, the ambling giant who has often been compared with Tate. He had a good strong action and the heart to match it so that he, like Tate, could keep going at full fast-medium pace much longer than the more recent quickies, who have had to waste time in order to conserve their energy. His overs averaged 2½ minutes each. Similar bowlers in the early 'eighties averaged not much short of five minutes.

Bradman considered Bedser a better bowler than Tate, who was 33 when he first bowled to the Don at his youthful best. Bradman was 18 years older when he first faced Bedser. The verdict might not have been so emphatically in Alec's favour if Bradman had met Tate at his zenith in 1924. They were both great bowlers and it is very difficult to separate them. Bedser did find a chink in the hitherto almost impenetrable Bradman defences in 1948, when he was not quite so quick on his feet and in his reactions. Bedser had his wicket in each of his first four Test innings, but at a cost, for the Don made 265 in those knocks. Late in-swing aided by safe hands at short leg was the usual form of dismissal.

The two great bowlers did not have very much in common, except their pace and the course of their careers. Tate was an instinctive bowler. He confessed that, whereas he was aware of how he swung the new ball, his away movement off the pitch with the older ball just seemed to happen. If he did not know when that was going to happen, the batsman had no chance of being forewarned. Bedser was a thinking bowler, who knew how he achieved his effects. Among his weapons was a leg-break at unchanged speed. Many called it a cutter, but Alec definitely spun it, and sometimes it turned surprisingly against the odds. On the shirt-front Adelaide pitch in 1947 he suddenly produced one which moved just enough to bowl Bradman for a duck.

It was curious how the careers of the two moved in parallel. Both were handicapped by lost war years, for the Bedsers were preparing to force their way into the Surrey side in 1939. Thus they both came to Test cricket in their late twenties. They both toured Australia three times and both set records, Tate with 38 wickets on tour in 1924–25, and Bedser with 39 at home in 1953. Bedser's record was broken three years later when Laker had his fantastic series with 46 wickets, including 19 in the Manchester Test. Finally, the closing stages of their Test careers were similar.

Tate in 1932 and Bedser in 1954 toured Australia without having definite parts to play in the attacks based on maximum speed. Jardine in 1932 had Larwood, Voce, Allen and Bowes. Tate did not fit into his plans and was not among the original selections. That he toured at all was almost entirely due to a weightily mounted press campaign. Much the same happened to Bedser in 1954, when Hutton's strategy was based on the expresses of Frank Tyson and Brian Statham, with Bailey as supporting fast-medium stock-bowler. Because Hutton miscalculated at Brisbane, where he played four pace-bowlers without either of his spinners, Bob Appleyard and Johnny Wardle, Alec did play in the first Test but not again. Both times the skipper's tactics brought overwhelming victories; Tate and Bedser were disappointed but had no grievance.

14
Changes – for the better?

To understand cricket in the first half of the century it is necessary to understand also what life generally was like, for that is reflected in games playing. Britain was essentially a clean and wholesome country, so law abiding that we even observed the many 'Keep Off The Grass' notices in parks and gardens. Crime was the possession of relatively few professionals, and we did not need to lock our cars. There was no mugging, and the threat of the 'cat' kept down other crimes of violence. Drug taking was so uncommon that an individual addict, Brenda Dean Paul, received wide publicity. Unemployment was unfortunately high, but I would willingly relive the 'thirties even though I had a tough freelancing year after being heaved out of the *Mirror*.

Cricket then reflected a wholesome way of life; hence the amateur spirit in which it was played. It reflected current life and attracted large crowds. For the Whitsun match at Lord's between Middlesex and Sussex, Portman, a great caterer who had the best bakery of North London in the old Tavern buildings, catered for 30,000 crowds. More than 80,000 watched Surrey v. Yorkshire in 1906. Twenty years later more than 40,000 sardined into Old Trafford to see Yorkshire one day, of whom 38,000 paid at the gate.

161

There was more individuality about cricketers of the first half of the century, who provided Tom Webster with his cartoon characters. Subsequently players tended to copy each other's mannerisms. It seems that 99.9 per cent of tennis players now bounce the ball several times before serving. Half of them surely do not know why. The same habit cannot suit everyone. At one time Bowes was having trouble with his run-up and tried a dummy run before opening the bowling. He then took seven wickets and, being superstitious, continued dummying. Before the war he did so alone. Afterwards he had hordes of imitators. Nearly every bowler did his dummy run before every spell, wasting so much time that legislation became necessary to check the habit. It would do nothing for me and, I am sure, most other bowlers.

Then we saw the crouching umpires. Frank Chester had been crouching for 20 years without attracting many others to the practice. Soon after the war nearly all umpires, creaking ancients among them, crouched until a new trend-setter returned to the upright stance and enabled them to straighten their backs.

Cricketers have become slaves of fashion, reflecting life in a much changed Britain. The embarrassing habit of embracing each other whenever a wicket falls is the most jarring. In my time bowlers expected wickets and took them in their stride. Helmets, too, are largely a habit. Accomplished batsmen should have the footwork to keep their heads out of trouble, and others should be able to move aside from bouncers. In more than half a century I have seen very very few batsmen hit directly on the head. I would hate the handicap of a load on my head. Thigh pads are also a quite needless encumbrance. Because pictures show batsmen between the wars obviously without such pads – Hobbs and Sutcliffe going to the wicket for example – it is now assumed that they had not been invented. They had but were not in great demand. A right-hander can wear one on the outside of the left thigh, which is seldom hit and then not very painfully. The painful and more frequent blow is on the inside of the other thigh, where a pad would impede running.

The Victorians who framed the laws and conditions for cricket were wiser than their successors. They bequeathed a well-ordered game, and it was long recognised that only minor changes might become necessary occasionally. Enlarging the wicket in the 'thirties was one. Tinkering with the lbw law was a major move, the forerunner of many. Logic might dictate a change, but cricket is full of illogicalities, notably leg-byes. The change, which brought balls pitched outside the off stump into lbw consideration, was itself illogical, for it ignored those pitched as worthily to leg. Charlie Barnett said he was affected essentially by the loss of an attacking stroke. Instead of putting his right leg across and playing a forcing stroke, he was compelled to play shortish balls near the off stump defensively.

I never saw merit in most subsequent changes. Some were aimless; others did not have the desired result. One was a law requiring that the fielder making a catch should not afterwards carry the ball outside the boundary. If he did, the batsman, having been caught, was to be awarded six runs! A particularly fine deep-field catch I saw was by Sid Brown for Middlesex at The Oval. He was long-on at the Vauxhall end. When the left-handed Fishlock hit high towards the scoreboard, he ran far and fast, made the catch at full speed some five yards inside the boundary and came to rest as many yards outside it. When is a brilliant catch no catch? Ask modern legislators.

The question could not have arisen before the war, when the entire playing area of the grounds was in play. Shortened artificial boundaries lay ahead. At The Oval in 1919 Hobbs and Jack Crawford ran seven for a shot towards Vauxhall, in the course of hitting 96 in 32 minutes to beat Kent.

The 75-yard boundary was designed to encourage the hitting of sixes; instead it incited bowlers to be negative. A mini-ground is no inducement to a slow bowler to keep a full length. The no-ball law change was similarly needless and produced farcical episodes. Moreover, its inefficient drafting caused it to be amended twice. The craze for change embraced most aspects of the game, not least the County Championship, whose new bonus points system has been counter-productive. Remembering how long we waited after Churchill for a Prime Minister with the courage of her convictions, men's cricket perhaps should seek guidance from the Women's Cricket Association!

Modern changes have upset other games also. Rugger was satisfying enough when few players could kick the heavy leather ball well. It was a handling game with emphasis on the scoring of tries. Now a ball which flies much further and players who have learned to kick have transformed it into a rather stupid penalty-kicking contest. Ireland scored no tries against Scotland, but Campbell kicked seven goals to make sure of the 1982 championship. Hardly a satisfying result.

Hockey has been damaged by the short Indian stick. The ball is now played much closer to the body than with the longer British stick, and there is much more reverse stick play. Hence we have more obstruction, leading to more whistling by umpires, and instead of flowing, hockey has become a stop-go-stop affair.

Modern changes have tended to sap the sporting nature of games. As far as possible chance has been eliminated to cater for commercially-minded players. The stymie, an exciting feature of match-play, has been banished from golf, and so have blind holes, including short ones at Sandwich and Deal, which used to be great fun. Eliminate chance, suppress fun, and games lose their sporting character. They may also become farcical – deciding an unsettled encounter by tossing a coin, or penalty-spot kicks to decide football games.

Cricket's post-war rulers dabbled in pitch preparation to such an extent that we endured a period of rough tracks followed by water-meadow pitches, so grassy that the ball's seam did the work for the bowler. Before one Essex match Bailey asked Laker to have a look at the pitch. He was long away and explained, 'I was looking for the pitch.'

Before the war and for a time afterwards groundsmen were

merely instructed to prepare the best possible pitches. That meant removing the greenery, using clay substances and the huge roller weighing several tons, which was slowly propelled by ten or eleven straining men. It did a job beyond the scope of the briskly moving motorised roller of today. The result was pitches both fast and true. Soon instructions came from Lord's to switch from clay to Surrey loam, good stuff for flowers but without binding qualities, and surface grass was needed as a binder. Clays, which include the red Nottingham marl, were discouraged because they dry more slowly than loam, which is quite immaterial when pitches are completely covered.

Marl, sometimes mixed with cow manure, as at Lord's, was an ingredient of most top dressings in my playing time. Excellent pitches demanded all the bowling arts and variations, and the game moved briskly on the fast grounds. Leyton was notably quick in the middle and barren in the outfield. After Kennedy bowled the first over of a match there, the other Hampshire bowler was mauled by Laurie Eastman. The ball was already whiskery. Kennedy let it dangle from a leather sliver and asked Tom Pearce, the other Essex batsman, how he would fancy being a new-ball bowler at Leyton.

The arrival of TV was initially a calamity for cricket. Formerly enthusiasts had to visit grounds to see how Hobbs and Bradman, Hammond and Hutton, Compton and McCabe looked and played. Soon Boycott and Botham, Richards and Chappell, Lillee and Holding could be studied from an armchair at home. The first match televised from Old Trafford was Winston Place's benefit, and the Saturday gate was so reduced that Lancashire granted him compensation of £1,000, a large sum at the time. Later the BBC paid handsomely for TV and radio rights, but by then cricket in desperation had sold its soul to a new audience enamoured of the stultifying limited-overs scramble.

Another innovation liable to be counter-productive was the issuing of light meters to umpires. The human eye, not a box of tricks, has to watch the ball. The most important factor is usually not the degree of light but the background. Only once did I bat

165

when the background in dull light justified coming off, but in circumstances which did not justify an appeal. During a Cross Arrows game against United Hospitals at Lord's, on the main ground late in September, our seventh wicket fell just over 15 minutes before time, and that seemed to me to rule out appealing. Two more wickets fell, but we just held out. The light has to be very bad to justify stopping, even against fast bowling. After he retired Leyland was asked how often appeals had been justified in matches he played. 'Never,' he said, adding that the appeals had invariably been tactical.

In my experience the light was most often difficult when the sun was shining. Glossy white paint was formerly used instead of today's matt finish, notably on sight-screens. At Lord's the sight-screen was flanked by glossy white seats on the top deck of the Mound, and the sun shimmering from the mass of whiteness was a batting worry. It was preferable to face the pavilion, where there was then no sight-screen, and the same was true of The Oval, although there that meant looking into a black background. A canvas awning used to stretch from the balcony to high supports close to the field of play. Yet I never had the slightest difficulty in seeing the ball against the gloom beneath. The Oval dressing room attendant in the early years of the century owed his nickname to the awning. A careless member on the balcony tossed a cigarette, which caused the canvas to smoulder and spring a leak. Along came the attendant with a bucket of water, flooded the embryo fire and the top-hatted member sitting below and became known as Fireman Read.

A vital influence on the changing face of cricket has been commercialism. Many years ago Jack Hobbs remarked that cricket's trouble – trouble even then – was that there was too much money in it. Test players were then paid £60 a match. What would he say now, when they collect £1,400? The modern player can earn in a single day as much as Hobbs ever did for a full series just by sitting in the pavilion until shortly after tea on the first day, watching the earlier batsmen perform.

Unfortunately, the more they are paid, the smaller is the quantity of cricket they provide.

Another feature of cricket, indeed of all sport, which is not good for the game is the dual role of leading players as performers and critics of fellow performers. Team spirit is not improved. After Percy Fender and Rockley Wilson wrote from Australia about the 1920–21 MCC tour for newspapers in England, which caused ill-feeling, players were barred from similar activities. More than 30 years later Trevor Bailey lost his chance of captaining England, because he included a chapter in a book about his too-recent tour of the West Indies. Now the lessons of the past are forgotten, or ignored, and we may expect further ill-feeling.

It is sad to see a game slipping, but most spectators in the 'eighties have known only the game as now played. They seem to go along with crude behaviour of leading players. They accept their wild and embarrassing transports of delight when a wicket is taken – something totally unexpected? They seem indifferent to the great over-rate slowdown. Apparently falling playing standards, eroded by the limited-overs scrambles, do not deter them. And they are now the folk who matter and have to be considered.

They can certainly come back at me with the claim that they watch very good fielding. There has certainly been a large improvement. The difference is not among the best fielders, for those of the past, particularly the men within cover point distance of the wicket, were the equals of the experts of the 'eighties, but among the lesser lights. There is now much less difference between the best fielder and the worst in the side. Indeed to use the word 'worst' is a slur on the least skilled, when the general standard is so high. The rabbit fielder, who had to be hidden, is a man of the past. At one time he even forced his way into the Test side. Moreover virtually all modern fielders are versatile. Nobody has to be kept in one place, as was the case as recently as the 'sixties. The cumbersome heavyweight Colin Milburn was adequate at forward short leg. There came a time at Trent Bridge, however, when the England bowlers were being hammered by the West Indies, and most of the close positions had to be vacated. Milburn found his way to the deep field near the sightscreen, and Gary Sobers and partner ran a three, when he had to move a few yards to field the ball.

If conditions could be re-created in which young cricketers could develop their talents fully, the batting and bowling would again match the fielding. There is as much talent as there ever was, as I know from doing some coaching in Basingstoke. In addition to cricketers of 13 and 14 there was a sturdy little fellow in the nets aged 12, who is a natural games player. His instinctive batting should be only watched by a coach to see that he does not develop bad habits, for he should not suffer coaching interference. As a bowler he had a skip approaching the wicket. He cured that immediately he was shown how to do so. He bowled fast – for his age – or off-breaks. I asked if he could also bowl a leg-break, and he promptly bowled one that pitched around the leg stump, beat the young batsman and missed the off stump. Because I have known too many leg-spinners, whose method is a strain, particularly on the right shoulder, come to grief before their bones and muscles are set, I advised this youngster to keep his leg-break on ice for the next six or seven years.

I shall probably not see whether he graduates to the highest class, as his talents suggest. I can but hope that he will not suffer too much from having to play too many stultifying games in which each side is restricted to 20 overs. Nothing could be devised more damaging to youngsters.

My sympathy goes to the current outstanding batsmen, Viv Richards, Greg Chappell and company. They deserve sympathy, because they have to display their skill in such a limited field. They bat almost exclusively against seam bowling, fast and medium, and a few slower orthodox spinners with flat trajectories. They have no chance to evoke comparison with the Hobbs and Bradmans of the past by exploiting their skill against all types of bowling. We do not know if they would be as outstanding against leg-spinners and orthodox spinners armed with all the arts and guiles of flight and variation. Leg-spin almost vanished from Test cricket when Richie Benaud retired, and artful off-spin went with Fred Titmus, for the emphasis then switched from the taking of wickets to restricting the scoring. It is even longer since Tony Lock was the last left-hander practising the arts.

One feature of cricket has not seemingly changed. Selectors are still erratic, as the treatment of Mike Gatting illustrates. He has suffered as Gunn, Bowes, Paynter, Bill Edrich, Robertson and Jackson did. Here is a young batsman who looks technically better equipped than any other among the younger Englishmen except Graham Gooch, and who has proved himself against Australia. In seven Tests against our major opponents he has played five innings of more than 50. Yet previously in the West Indies he was ignored by the captain, Ian Botham, and immediately after success against Australia he was demoted by Keith Fletcher from his position from third to fifth wicket down and eased out of the Test side. Then at the start of 1982 a new selection committee under a new chairman, Peter May, ignored him, although England's two leading batsmen, Boycott and Gooch, were not available for selection.

In one sense players of the past and present stand at opposite poles. Today they carry the weight, helmets, on their heads. We used to carry it on our feet. A case of pressure on the corns instead of on the brain. We wore two or three pairs of thick woollen socks in stout boots, which gave our ankles good support. The modern lightweight shoes, often with rubber soles, clearly help fielders to be acrobatic, but the lack of ankle support is a threat to batsmen and bowlers. In his last Test against Australia Ray Illingworth, wearing modern lightweights, turned and sprained an ankle, and his absence on a pitch requiring spin contributed to an England defeat. A decade later Frank Hayes of Lancashire broke an ankle while turning for a second run.

Meanwhile, my generation may happily look back on

pleasingly fast-moving matches and undemonstrative cricketers who were dignified both on and off the field, without the disturbing recollection of someone like Lillee kicking an opponent and MCC members assaulting umpires. We recall orderly crowds who kept quiet while the ball was being bowled and played. We remember grounds with much of their original beauty and character before the concrete invasion. Viewed from the nursery end, Lord's had much more charm before the Q and Warner Stands were erected. The pavilion was flanked by low, single-deck stands. The south wall of the pavilion was ivy-covered, like the south clock-tower matching the one which still stands on the north side. It was victim of the newest concrete affair, the Tavern Stand, which also deprived us of the attractive old Tavern. Vast building projects, and each reduced the capacity of the ground! The Lord's record of some 34,000 is a distant memory, far beyond the ground's present capacity.

For the game's decline ruling bodies must accept much blame. Their greatest weakness has been their tendency to sway in the breeze of political expedience. Something more than swaying marked their actions in the matter of South Africa; they were blown flat. We worship democracy with its built-in compromise, but it must be admitted that cricket was much more settled when autocratic rulers, who were not given to compromise, abounded in the counties. Lord Hawke, Lord Harris, Peter Higson, John Daniel, and their like did not sway expediently.

My firm belief is that cricket reached its peak before the Great War. Only the Golden Age could accommodate a Sussex bowler from Australia, who was grandson of a rebel Irish chieftain and named so improbably as John Elicius Benedict Bernard Placid Quirk Carrington Dwyer. He was a professional, and the scorecards of the time did not therefore have the problem of fitting in J. E. B. B. P. Q. C. Dwyer.

My refuge is memory, including that of a splendidly militant Essex batsman, Canon F. H. Gillingham – the initial 'G' pronounced hard, unlike the town in Kent – who was among the very best after-dinner speakers and was said to be the only preacher who 'drew a gate'. Week after week he filled his church in the city. In September 1945 the Lord Mayor gave a dinner in the Mansion House to mark his seventieth birthday. I was invited, apparently because I knew him well. Gilly told us about his first match against Yorkshire. He drove a four through the covers, and 'I thought I was in Heaven'. He paused. 'I just hope Heaven will last longer next time.' And we may similarly hope that cricket will somehow come to another Golden Age, which, like Gilly's second Heaven, will last long. A pipe dream? Not necessarily, for it is not entirely true that life cannot put its clock back. Cricket put its back more than a century when admitting bookmakers to its grounds in the 'sixties. The past contains much that is far more worthy of restoration.

Index